PLAIN WRITTEN ENGLISH

for Business and Technical Applications

MAIN TEXT

Dr. Peter M. Skaer

BABEL UNIVERSITY
Professional School of Translation

Copyright © 2014 by Peter M. Skaer

Published by Babel Press USA
All rights reserved.

No part of this book may be used, reproduced, stored in a retrieval system, or transmitted, in any from or by any means, electric, mechanical, photocopying, recording, or otherwise, without the prior written permission of the author except in the case of brief quotations embodies in critical articles and reviews.

This book was originally a textbook for
"Plain Written English For Business And Technical Applications"
in Babel University Professional School of Translation programs

Written by Peter M. Skaer
Director Tomoki Hotta
Stylish editing by Yuko Yoshida
Cover design by Yuko Yoshida

ISBN-10:0-9836402-6-2
ISBN-13:978-0-9836402-6-4

Babel Corporation
Pacific Business News Bldg. #208,
1833 Kalakaua Avenue,
Honolulu, Hawaii 96815

Phone: (808) 946 - 3773
Fax: (808) 946 - 3993

Website: www.babel.edu
            http://www.babel.co.jp/usa/

Table of Contents

Foreword vii

PLAIN WRITTEN ENGLISH: Principles of Style and Composition
Principles of Plain Written English
Overview 8

I. Principle of Cohesiveness
Overview 10
A. Word Level Rules
  a. Conform to Context
  (1) Use Context to Determine Best Word Choice 12
  b. Be Consistent
  (2) Choose Words from Same Level of Formality 14
  (3) Avoid Mixing Common Words with Technical Ones 16
B. Sentence Level Rules
  a. Conform to Context
  (4) Use Present Tense, Active Voice, First Person Singular Whenever Possible ... 18
  b. Use a Logical Order
  (5) Use Basic Subject-Verb-Object (S-V-O) Word Order 20
  (6) Avoid Passive, Causative and Conditional Structures 22
  (7) Place Prepositions Correctly in Parallel Structures 24
  c. Be Consistent
  (8) Keep Tense the Same in Parallel Structures 26
  (9) Keep Types of Words the Same 28
  (10) Keep Degrees of Adjectives the Same 30
  d. Avoid Distractions
  (11) Avoid Overly Simple Structures by Combining Simple Sentences ... 32
  (12) Avoid Perfect and Subjunctive Tenses 34
C. Paragraph Level Rules
  a. Conform to Context
  (13) Know the Intended Audience, and Write to It 36
  (14) Choose a Design and Stick to It 38
  (15) Use the Correct Articles (A, An, The) 40
  b. Use a Logical Order
  (16) Organize Material Logically by Linking Paragraphs 42

(17) Begin a Paragraph with a Good Topic Sentence 44
  (18) Using Facts and Statistics in Supporting Statements 46
  (19) Using Examples and Lists as Supporting Statements 48
  (20) Using Opinions as Supporting Statements 50
  (21) Making Statements of Comparison and Contrast 52
  (22) Using the Cause and Effect Sequence 54
  (23) Making Clear Transitions within a Paragraph 56
  (24) Summarizing Your Points 58
  (25) Emphasizing Your Points 60
 c. Be Consistent
  (26) Avoid Shifts in Person 62
  (27) Avoid Shifts in Number 64
  (28) Avoid Shifts in Voice 66
  (29) Avoid Shifts in Tense 68
  (30) Avoid Shifts in Subject 70
  (31) Keep References, Labels, Units of Measurement Consistent ...72
 d. Avoid Distractions
  (32) Avoid Needless Repetition of Words 74

II. Principle Of Directness
 Overview 76
 A. Word Level Rules
  a. State What Things Are, Not What They Seem to Be
   (33) Use Concrete Terms 78
   (34) Avoid Lexical Ambiguity 80
  b. State the Subject Clearly
   (35) Avoid Indirect and Unspecific Subject and Object Reference ...82
 B. Sentence Level Rules.
  a. State What Things Are, Not What They Seem to Be
   (36) State What Things Are, Not What They Seem to Be............84
   (37) Avoid Syntactic Ambiguity..86
  b. State the Subject Clearly
   (38) Replace Adverbial and Adjectival Phrases with Single Adverbs and Adjectives....88
   (39) Using Scope to Avoid Misplaced Adverbs..............................90
   (40) Avoid Subject Ambiguity by Using the Correct Personal Pronouns............92
   (41) Avoid Subject and Object Ambiguity by Using Reflexive Pronouns Correctly...............94
  c. Avoid Negatives Whenever Possible

      (42) Avoid Negative Expressions and Double Negatives 96
  C. Paragraph Level Rules.
    a. State What Things Are, Not What They Seem to Be
      (43) Avoid Overstatement and Exaggeration 98
      (44) Separate Fact from Opinion 100
    b. State the Subject Clearly
      (45) Avoid Mixing Subjects and Objects up 102
      (46) Focus on the Message by Placing the Writer in the Background 104
    c. State the "Bottom Line" Succinctly
      (47) Avoid Developing Ideas that You Intend to Dismiss Later ...106
    d. Avoid Negatives Whenever Possible
      (48) Avoid Spite and Sarcasm 108
      (49) Be Direct, but Not Too Direct 110

III. Principle Of Economy.
  Overview 112
  A. Word Level Rules.
    a. Brief is Best: Using a Few Key Words Correctly is Better than Using a Lot of Words Incorrectly
      (50) Use Words You Know 114
    b. Common Words Are Preferred over Uncommon Words
      (51) Use Common Words Instead of Uncommon Specialty Words 116
      (52) Define/Gloss Special, New and Unknown Terms, Acronyms, and Expressions ...118
      (53) Avoid Coining New Words and Phrases 120
  B. Sentence Level Rules.
    a. Brief is Best: Fewer Words in a Sentence are Preferred to Expanded or Extended Narratives
      (54) Restrict Length of Sentences 122
      (55) Keep Sentences Separate in Ambiguous Situations 124
      (56) Avoid Restatement and Redundancy 126
      (57) Avoid Wordiness (Replace Wordy Phrases with Precise Terms) 128
      (58) Use Mainly Nouns and Verbs 130
      (59) Avoid Overuse and Misuse of Adjectives 132
      (60) Avoid Overuse and Misuse of Adverbs 134
    b. Avoid Subordinate Clauses
      (61) Avoid Reported Speech 136
      (62) Using Subordinate Conjunctions (Who, Which & That) 138
      (63) Using When and While as Conjunctions 140
    c. Discuss One Point Per Statement

      (64) Avoid Run-on Sentences 142
      (65) Avoid Unrelated Ideas in the Same Sentence 144
  C. Paragraph Level Rules.
    a. Brief is Best: Fewer Sentences are Preferred to Expanded Discourse
      (66) Underwrite, Rather than Overwrite 146
      (67) Be Brief and Concise: Break Writing into Short Sections 150
    b. Discuss One Point Per Statement
      (68) Develop Your Discussion One Step at a Time by Working from the Known to the Unknown ... 152

IV. Principle Of Appropriateness.
  Overview 154
  A. Word Level Rules.
    a. Be Truthful and Show Politeness and Respect for Others
      (69) Use Appropriate Gender References 156
      (70) Use Neutral Words 158
    b. Avoid Idioms and Slang, Especially the More Obscure Regional Variations
      (71) Avoid Colloquialism, Clichés, Slang and Regional Expressions 160
    c. Avoid Contractions and Casual Speech Rules
      (72) Avoid Uncommon Contractions... 162
  B. Sentence Level Rules.
    a. Be Truthful and Show Politeness and Respect for Others
      (73) Tell the Truth 164
      (74) Avoid Sweeping Generalizations and Stereotyping 166
      (75) Avoid Sexist, Racist and Prejudiced Comments 168
    b. Use Grammatically Correct Sentences
      (76) Keep Tense and Number in Agreement 170
      (77) Choosing Prepositions 174
      (78) Avoid Dangling Modifiers 176
      (79) Avoid Incomplete Sentences 178
  C. Paragraph Level Rules.
    a. Be Truthful and Show Politeness and Respect for Others.
      (80) Use Neutral Tone: Avoid Inference and Implication 180

Foreword

This text is both a resource for professional writers, and a tool for developing professional writing skills for newcomers as well as practitioners in the field. Though this text was originally written specifically for Japanese professionals who are writing English as a Second Language, it is in fact useful for all beginning, intermediate and advanced writers of all language backgrounds. This is the main text which includes complete explanations and illustrated examples for all 80 rules employed in the system of Plain Written English that is advocated here. In addition, there is a companion text, *Plain Written English for Business and Technical Applications Workbook*, which includes exercise sets for all 80 chapters contained in this volume, with suggested "model" answers available online. While both texts may be used independently, it is highly recommended that both texts be employed together in order to maximize the benefits for your own writing needs.

I. PLAIN WRITTEN ENGLISH: PRINCIPLES OF STYLE AND COMPOSITION.

Principles of Plain Written English
Overview

When we are in a situation where we must use a language other than our native language, it is particularly important to make sure that what we are writing is truly what we want to communicate. We want our message to be understood clearly and precisely. In the case of English, of course this means that we need to use the basic rules of grammar correctly. However, it also means that we need to organize, or direct, our writing so that it is unambiguous. In essence, we need to pay attention to language usage rules, in addition to simply being aware of the grammar (and culture) of the language. Language usage rules combine culture, grammar and common sense into a systematic approach to using a second language. For English, we have called this approach the "Plain English" approach. In effect, the Plain English approach provides usage guidelines for the basic grammatical rules of English, with the objective of producing plain unambiguous language from the English-as-a-second-language user.

Plain English is particularly important in on-the-job professional situations. In the workplace, where precision and clarity is essential, we must sometimes simplify our text so that our messages are plain and direct representations of what we want to communicate. So, in order to learn to write Plain English for the workplace, some professionals need to acquire a better understanding of the basic rules of English grammar and usage, while others need to simplify and refine their use of the English language. For these writers, and the others that fall in between, I have developed a set of ***Plain English Principles***.

The ***Plain English Principles*** are guidelines by which to help the writer understand how to communicate clearly and effectively in English. There are four basic principles; ***the Principle of Cohesiveness, the Principle of Economy, the Principle of Directness and the Principle of Appropriateness***. These principles are meant to supplement the basic grammatical rules of English, which are basically structural guidelines for building sentences. Each of these principles is supported and illustrated by several rules. The rules work together to help guide the production of Plain English, providing a systematic approach to effective English communication. These four principles comprise a system of effective language usage, and are designed to assist writers in developing clear plain English text that is appropriate for business, technical and other professional applications. These principles can be applied, of course, to general writing purposes where the goals of clarity, brevity and concreteness are similarly embraced.

So, while complex grammatical structures such as subordinate or relative clauses might be perfectly correct examples of English grammar, the Principles of both Economy and Directness would discourage the writer from using these structures in written English. For another example, one Plain English rule is "Discuss only one fact per statement (Principle of Economy)." This rule is quite useful when you are describing a new product with many features, some of which are new, others old. When you are writing about a new product, for example, it will be much clearer for your audience if you take each feature one at a time, step by step, perhaps building in terms of importance and impact as you go, rather than combining references to several features all in one sentence. The Principles of Plain English, then, are principles that guide the writer towards clear and effective writing, helping the writer to use the rules of English in a natural and straightforward way.

I. PRINCIPLE OF COHESIVENESS

Overview

The ***Principle of Cohesiveness*** is composed of four basic rules. These rules are: 1) Conform to Context; 2) Be Consistent; 3) Use a Logical Order, and; 4) Avoid Distractions. In essence, the Principle of Cohesiveness helps us to tie our ideas together into well-formed units. So, words are combined into well-formed phrases, phrases into well-formed sentences and sentences into well-formed paragraphs. The Principle of Cohesiveness unifies our thoughts around a central idea, or structure, and helps us to move from one point to another in a clear and understandable fashion. It organizes our words along standard forms of writing, and helps the audience move smoothly through the various points of our discussion. Each of the rules that make up this Principle is naturally connected to one another, and serve to reinforce and clarify the Principle that they represent.

The first rule of the Principle of Cohesiveness is ***Conform to Context***. In the following pages we employ this rule at the word, sentence and paragraph levels or writing. Before we write even a single word, it is important to determine why we are writing, what we are writing, and to whom we are writing. In essence, it is important to determine who the audience is, how much the audience knows about the subject, how they think about the subject, and what they need to learn from you. Context determines how formal or informal your writing is, how technical or colloquial your expressions are, how detailed or general your observations are, and finally, how you approach the subject.

The second rule of the Principle of Cohesiveness is ***Use a Logical Order***. We see this rule employed at two levels of writing: the sentence level and the paragraph level. What exactly constitutes a logical order is in part determined by the target language (English) and in part by the context in which the writing will be used. For normal English writing, the logical order is simply the order of words in a straightforward declarative statement, with the subject first, verb second and object (if included) third. Additionally, various types of writing require writers to follow a specific format, or sequence, in order to introduce facts, opinions, points and counterpoints. These sequences are illustrated in this section.

The third rule of the Principle of Cohesiveness, **Be Consistent**, is used at all three levels of writing: the word level; the sentence level, and; the paragraph level. Again, this rule is also related to context. Once an appropriate context is determined, and a format decided upon, it is essential to stay within the parameters that you have determined for yourself. We don't want to mix degrees of formality, technical levels of vocabulary and structural aspects of sentences such as tense, and so forth. Once we have an overall design, it is best to stick to it throughout the entire text.

The fourth rule of the Principle of Cohesiveness is to **Avoid Distractions**. This rule is used at both the sentence and paragraph levels of writing, and helps us to keep our writing style and structure from intruding upon the points that we are making. We don't want our writing form itself to become the focus of our readers, rather, we want them to focus on the content. Distractions can come in many forms, from writing in overly simplistic prose, to writing simple ideas in overly complex ways. In Plain Written English, we want to focus on presenting ideas in clear uncluttered fashion, in ways that will direct the readers' attention to the specific points we wish them to consider, and have them consider these points free of unnecessary concern or distraction as a result of poor writing style.

I. PRINCIPLE OF COHESIVENESS – A. WORD LEVEL.
a. CONFORM TO CONTEXT

(1)   Use Context to Determine Best Word Choice.

The words you use largely depend upon your intended audience. If you are writing a memo to your secretary, asking him to look after some business, your writing style and word choice will likely be informal. However, if you are writing a note to a management representative, asking to be considered for promotion to a recently vacated position, your style and word choice will likely be more formal. More importantly, though, this rule is governed by the context in which it is used. In other words, in a very small organization, a letter to management might be informal, since you are familiar with the representative, perhaps even good friends with the individual. On the other hand, the secretary you are leaving a note for may be a replacement for your regular secretary, and thus not familiar to you at all. In such a situation, it is best to put a little distance between yourselves, and adopt a semi-formal writing style and word choice.

The key here is to use words and style that fit the situation. The situation is closely related to how familiar the people are to whom you are writing the message. The more familiar the audience, the more informal the word choice. When the audience is outside of the group that you would consider your own personal friends, then it is best to use a semi-formal style, and use words that are common to the field you are addressing, but are not excessively intimate, casual or familiar.

There are some expressions that are left over from a more formal era of communication, when communications were hand-written and style was emphasized. Expressions from this period include "As per your request," "Enclosed herewith," "beg to inform," "Pursuant to our conversation," and so forth. In general, avoid overly formal and archaic expressions in all situations by using clear straightforward language.

Examples.

Bad: As per your request, I am currently delving into the issues raised in your letter of 12 December, 2012.

Good: **I am looking into the questions you raised in your December 12, 2012 letter.**

Bad: Pursuant to our conversation of December 24, 2012, I am enclosing copies of all transactions between our firm and yours for the period of fiscal year 2012.

Good: **Following up on our conversation of December 24, 2012, I am enclosing copies of all transactions between our firm and yours for the 2012 fiscal year.**

Bad: Mary, dear, can you give my application some consideration for the opening in sales?

Good: **I would appreciate it if you would consider my application for the opening in the sales department.**

Bad: Dear sir, I would be forever humbled if you would be so kind as to respond favorably to my request for an extended leave of absence from your highly esteemed company.

Good: **I hope that you will be able to grant my request for an extended leave of absence.**

I. PRINCIPLE OF COHESIVENESS – A. WORD LEVEL.
b. BE CONSISTENT

(2)   Choose Words from the Same Level of Formality.

Once you have determined the context that you are writing in (see Rule #1), it is important to stay within the confines of that level throughout the entire text. Basically we determine an appropriate level of usage, and use terms that conform to that level. When in doubt as to what level of formality to use, it is best to use the somewhat detached semi-formal level for most of your writings. This level is used when your audience is not among your close inner circle of friends, but where the audience also does not require an obvious exaggerated degree of formality (as if you were writing a personal request to the Prime Minister of Japan, to the Canadian Ambassador, and so forth). Semi-formal style means that you employ words such as *please* and thank you *(Thank you in advance for your help in these matters)* rather than the more informal t*hanks (Thanks for your help)*, and for requests, conditionals such as *would* and *could (Could you look into these questions at your earliest possible convenience?)*, rather than making direct requests *(Look into these maters right away)*. We will see more examples of this neutral style of writing throughout the text.

The key point here to remember is that we want to avoid bringing in words that are more suitable for other levels, so that we <u>avoid the mixing of degrees of formality within a single text</u>. In other words, we want to avoid overly familiar references (such as using a person's first name) in an otherwise formal piece, or likewise, we want to avoid overly formal vocabulary (such as "the party in question" when referring to another person) in notes of a familiar and personal nature. Similarly, if we refer neutrally to certain things (using words such as "one"), then we need to avoid bringing in non-neutral terms (like "he" or "she"). To repeat, we want to avoid mixing usage levels, or degrees of formality, within a single text.

> Examples.

Bad: I thought I should let you know, Mary, that even though we have never met, I think it is important for management to increase the retirement benefits options for all employees at your firm.

Good: I think it is important for management to increase the retirement benefits options for all employees at your firm.

Bad: I spoke to the party in question the other day at lunch and she seemed quite willing to make a change, so let's do it.

Good: I spoke to Seiichi the other day at lunch and he seemed quite willing to make a change, so let's do it.

Bad: If one wishes to leave before the completion of his contract, he may be liable for non-completion of contract penalties.

Good: If he wishes to leave before the completion of his contract, he may be liable for non-completion of contract penalties.
(or)
Good: If one wishes to leave before the completion of the contract, there may be penalties for non-completion of the contract.

Bad: The magnitude of the problem is surely outweighed by the piddling nature of the consequences.

Good: The magnitude of the problem is surely outweighed by the trivial nature of the consequences.

I. PRINCIPLE OF COHESIVENESS – A. WORD LEVEL.
b. BE CONSISTENT

(3)   Avoid Mixing Common Words with Technical Ones.

The third rule illustrating the Principle of Cohesiveness continues the same theme introduced in Rules #1 and #2. Essentially, it is best not to mix two different types of vocabulary. First, we decide what level of usage is most appropriate for the intended audience. From our determination of the appropriate formality level, we then establish our writing in a frame of usage that contains a range of vocabulary. <u>Once we decide on a range of vocabulary, it is best to stay within the confines of this set</u>, rather than randomly accessing other sets at our whim.

When using professional terms, our decision regarding which range of vocabulary to use also determines whether we will use highly technical or professional terms, or whether we will use more common "layman" terms. Whichever set of expressions we choose to draw from, it is important, in order to maintain cohesiveness, to stay within this range. Whether you choose common references or technical jargon will ultimately depend on who the intended audience is.

To illustrate our point about not mixing the common with the technical, let us imagine a letter from an automobile parts distributor, we would not expect to find the writer mixing the following terms: (bad) "Our most popular car tire is the VR17 Dynamic Radial, designed for all-weather usage. This is the same tire that is *on the wheels of* all of Niyoda's top-of-the-line automobiles." Though a *wheel* refers to a part of an automobile, it is not a technical term on the same level as *radials, all weather usage,* and so forth. As such, this phrase *(on the wheels of)* is more suitably replaced by something like: (good) "Our most popular car tire is the VR17 Dynamic Radial, designed for all-weather usage. This is the same tire that is *included as standard equipment on* all of Niyoda's top-of-the-line automobiles."

> Examples.

Bad: Our company has just acquired a new ABM model V work station with a 896 processor and dual ROM drives. We haven't been able to get the thing that points to stuff on the screen to work.

Good: **Our company has just acquired a new ABM model V work station with a 896 processor and dual ROM drives. We haven't been able to get the cursor to operate correctly.**

Bad: I would like to introduce our new line of office supplies to you. Our products include copying paper, pens and pencils and high speed electronic graphite reducers.

Good: **I would like to introduce our new line of office supplies to you. Our products include copying paper, pens and pencils and electronic pencil sharpeners.**

Bad: We worked hard throughout all of last year to eventuate our leadership in the sales of small knick knacks.

Good: **We worked hard throughout all of last year to become the leader in the sales of small knick knacks.**

Bad: We are looking for employees who are meticulous in their work, courteous to customers and who like to be silly on occasion.

Better: **We are looking for employees who are meticulous in their work, courteous to customers and who have a humorous disposition.**

Best: We are looking for hard workers who are good with customers and have a sense of humor.

I. PRINCIPLE OF COHESIVENESS – B. SENTENCE LEVEL.
a. CONFORM TO CONTEXT

(4)   Use Present Tense, Active Voice, First Person Singular Whenever Possible.

The present tense is the best tense to use for most writing. It is clear and unencumbered, and is the established tense to use to talk about theories, hypotheses, beliefs, commonly held truths, facts and so forth. Rarely is the future tense needed (things either are, or they aren't), and the past tense is reserved exclusively to discuss past experiments, research or other events that clearly took place before the time of the writing.

Generally, we use the first person singular subject form as the writer. So, words such as "I" are used throughout the text, to indicate the author's "voice." Second person terms such as "you," or a person's name ("Bill") are used to refer to the person who is being addressed (the audience), while third person ("he," "she" and "it") are used to refer to the people or things being discussed. There is a tendency to sometimes use an impersonal voice, employing terms such as "one," but this is to be avoided in anything but the most formal writings (such as in contracts, but not in reports, academic writing, etc.). For the most part, it is best to avoid detached second and third person singular and plural voices. On the other hand, it is common to use the first person plural in some forms of writing, such as in this text, where the writer wishes to demonstrate a closeness, or degree of familiarity, with his audience. By using terms such as "we," the author associates himself with the audience, and in effect, identifies his mission as that of the audience, so that both the author and the audience appear to be working hand-in-hand towards the same goals. However, for most <u>business writings,</u> this degree of familiarity is not desired, so, the first person singular is preferred.

Using the active voice *(Igor bought a car)* is preferred over a passive voice *(A car was bought by Igor)* because the active voice is more direct and clear. It demonstrates that you are in charge of the situation, rather than passively hiding from responsibility. Passive reflects a degree of detachment and formality, and is likely to set you apart from your audience.

> Examples.

Bad: The new Niyoda 5000 will get about 30 miles to the gallon in the city and up to 50 miles to the gallon on the highway.

Good: The new Niyoda 5000 gets about 30 miles to the gallon in the city and up to 50 miles to the gallon on the highway.

Bad: Some design flaws in the new disposal system have been discovered.

Good: I have discovered that there are some design flaws in the new disposal system.

Bad: If one were to believe such a thing, one should probably find a different place to live.

Good: If you believed such a thing, you should probably find a different place to live.

Bad: In this report, we first will consider the best ways to dispose of the remaining inventory, and then we will look at possible solutions to updating the equipment.

Good: In this report I first consider the best ways to dispose of the remaining inventory, and then I review possible solutions to updating the equipment.

I. PRINCIPLE OF COHESIVENESS – B. SENTENCE LEVEL.
b. USE A LOGICAL ORDER

(5)   Use Basic Subject-Verb-Object (S-V-O) Word Order.

The basic order of words in English syntax is Subject-Verb-Object. This order is the one used in simple present tense active voice sentences, and is the clearest and most direct form of the English sentence. Japanese, on the other hand, employs a basic syntactic order of Subject-Object-Verb. Japanese who are writing English sometimes have a tendency to carry over the Japanese word order into their English writing. What happens is that the English syntax becomes overly complex, since it often requires using the passive, rather than the active voice. It is best to try to think in terms of S-V-O, since by doing so your sentences will become more direct, less cluttered, and or course, clearer.

When we have modifiers such as adverbs and adjectives, the modifiers fit into this basic S-V-O structure predictably. Generally, adjectives (the words that modify nouns), are placed <u>before</u> the nouns they modify (the adjective *new* goes before the noun *store*, to make the *new store*). Adverbs, on the other hand, can be placed at the beginning or the ends of sentences. An adverb such as *yesterday*, then, can go before or after a main sentence such as *I went to the amusement park (I went to the amusement park yesterday,* or, *Yesterday I went to the amusement park).* Prepositional phrases (which indicate direction of movement) are best placed after the main verb (and object). We will discuss in later sections how to deal with modifiers in more complex sentences, but for our purposes here, it is important simply to follow the basic Subject-Verb-Object sequence when you are writing clear business text.

Of course, there are exceptions to virtually every language rule. You may have already thought of some yourself. For example, what about questions in English? Certainly questions such as "Is it time to order new supplies?" and "Who do you work for?" seem to fall out of the basic sentence order described above. This is true to some extent, so it is important here to simply concentrate on the <u>basic form of statements</u> (Subject-Verb-Object), not questions, since in fact in English we do change the order for many questions, a topic we will deal with later in this text.

> Examples.

Bad: To the store went Michiko.

Good: Michiko went to the store.

Bad: His speech was heard by everyone.

Good: Everyone heard his speech.

Bad: Ken was asked by the boss to come see him.

Good: The boss asked Ken to come see him.

Bad: Rice was delivered to the store by a new distributor.

Good: A new distributor delivered rice to the store.

Bad: I believed him to be the man responsible for the turn around of the company profits.

Good: He is the man responsible for the company's increased profits.

Bad: On the way to the office I saw a building on fire.

Good: I saw a building on fire on the way to the office

Bad: Towards the staircase I walked.

Good: I walked towards the staircase.

I. PRINCIPLE OF COHESIVENESS – B. SENTENCE LEVEL.
b. USE A LOGICAL ORDER

(6)   Avoid Passive, Causative and Conditional Structures.

In this rule, we extend and clarify the ideas discussed in Rule (5), above. Specifically, we want to avoid types of structure that force us to deviate from the basic syntactic structure (such as passive, causative and conditional forms). For example, passives place the object in subject position, and the subject in object position (Active: *Igor wrote a letter.* Passive: *A letter was written by Igor.*)

Causatives, on the other hand, place a subject in a sentence which causes an action to take place. (Active/Causative: *The boss asked Igor to write a letter.*) While the last example is not very difficult, it is clear that it is indeed a more complex sentence than just the simple active example above. We have the main subject *(the boss)* causing an action to be performed by the subject of the active sentence *(Igor)*. In more complex discussions, this structure of "multiple subjects" can be confusing. If, for example, we made the causative statement in a passive voice, the resulting sentence takes more time to understand clearly (Passive/Causative: *The boss asked that a letter be written by Igor.*) This becomes even more difficult if we change tenses to the past, or even the future.

Similarly, conditional expressions (expressions using *if, unless*) can be confusing and misleading. For example, the sentence *If the applicant is qualified, I'll hire him* is fairly straightforward (we don't know yet if the applicant is qualified), but the sentence *If the applicant were more qualified, I'd hire him* is less straightforward (the applicant is not qualified), and even more confusing is the sentence *If I had known the applicant was qualified, I would have hired him* (the applicant was qualified, but not hired). In order to avoid the conditional, it is frequently necessary to change the overall structure of the sentence, as the last example below illustrates.

In general then, it is best to avoid passives, causatives and conditionals in favor of a more direct sentence structure, and certainly avoid mixing passives, causatives and conditionals together.

Examples.

Bad: The child was given a toy by the man.

Good: The man gave the child a toy.

Bad: The report was supposed to have been finished by Keiko by closing time.

Good: Keiko was supposed to have finished the report by closing time.

Bad: The supervisor demanded that lunch be eaten by the employees after they had finished their work.

Good: The supervisor demanded that the employees eat their lunch after they finished their work.

Bad: Being reprimanded in front of co-workers is embarrassing.

Good: It is embarrassing to be reprimanded in front of co-workers.

Bad: If I had known the applicant was qualified, I would have hired him.

Good: I didn't hire the applicant because I didn't think he was qualified.
(or)
Good: I would have hired him if he was qualified.

Bad: She could have had been given the promotion if she had just expressed some interest in the position.

Good: She did not show any interest in the position, so we gave someone else the job.

I. PRINCIPLE OF COHESIVENESS – B. SENTENCE LEVEL.
b. USE A LOGICAL ORDER

(7)   Placing Prepositions Correctly in Parallel Structures.

In sentences where prepositions are part of the phrases listed, you can either use the prepositions once at the beginning of the list, or you must include them with each member of the list (but not a mixture). A parallel structure is where there are two or more (usually dependent) clauses included in a sentence, where the clauses are in some sense equal to one another (we see this structure commonly in various types of lists). For example, the following sentences contain parallel structures involving prepositions.

I go to the university *on Mondays, Wednesdays and Fridays.*

I went to *the bookstore, the library and the post office,* but no one had copies of last year's tax forms.

In general, if the list is very long, it is best to use the preposition just once at the beginning before the items in parallel, in order to avoid unfavorable stylistic problems by repeating the same preposition over and over again. Further, it is important to keep things consistent by not including the preposition in some of the clauses (or phrases), but including it in others. Basically, then, the rule for preposition use is to use one with each phrase of the parallel items, or only before the first one of the series (and not a mixture of the two). The longer the list is, the more awkward the repetition of the prepositions become. If we were to reduce this to one simple rule of usage, then simply use the preposition once before the series of parallel phrases that it modifies.

> Examples.

Bad: The new paint can be used on metal, plastic, wood and on paper.

Good: The new paint can be used on metal, plastic, wood and paper.

Bad: We found moths in drawers, closets and even in boxes.

Good: We found moths in drawers, in closets and even in suitcases.
(or)
Good: We found moths in drawers, closets and even suitcases.

Bad: The original plan was developed by an amateur, but the final proposal was completed with a professional.

Good: The original plan was developed by an amateur, but the final proposal was completed by a professional.

Bad: The bar service begins at 6:00 PM, the buffet by 7:00 PM, and the awards ceremony at 8:00 PM.

Good: The bar service begins at 6:00 PM, the buffet at 7:00 PM, and the awards ceremony at 8:00 PM.

Bad: Malfunctions can be caused by poor workmanship, poor materials and by poor design.

Good: Malfunctions can be caused by poor workmanship, poor materials and poor design.

I. PRINCIPLE OF COHESIVENESS – B. SENTENCE LEVEL.
c. BE CONSISTENT

(8)   Keep the Tense the Same in Parallel Structures.

While we have suggested earlier that it is best to stick to the present tense in your business writing, it is important to also stick with the same forms of the tense. The present tense in English actually has several different forms. These include the *habitual present tense* (I eat, you eat, she eats), the progressive or continuative present tense (I am eating, you are eating, she is eating), and the *present perfect progressive tense* (I have been eating, you have been eating, she has been eating), among others. We will recommend later that you avoid the perfect tenses for clarity sake, but it is useful here to simply recognize that they do exist.

When a series of verbs are in a parallel construction in the same sentence, whether they are part of a sequence, part of a single statement, or part of a balanced observation, it is important that they all are of the same form (tense). To illustrate this you may recognize the following parallel structures:

"I *came*, I *saw*, I *conquered*." (attributed to Julius Caesar)

"*To be,* or not *to be,* that is the question." (from Shakespeare's Hamlet). In Caesar's example, we have a list of three verbs in a parallel construction, so they are all in the same tense (simple past). Likewise, in the Hamlet quote we see another example of a parallel construction, namely, two infinitives ("*to be*, or not *to be*"). Similarly, if you are listing verbs in the gerund form (the *-ing* form) then generally you want to keep all of the verbs in the same form.

"I like *singing, dancing* and *drinking* beer."

Further, if you are listing items of information, then frame each item in a similar structure (as noun phrases, as verb phrases, but not a mixture of both).

"*Walking* and *talking* alone in a park is not a crime."

"We just *ate* breakfast and *talked* over old times together."

| Examples. |

Bad: Writing in a foreign language is much easier than to speak a foreign language.

Good: Writing in a foreign language is much easier than speaking in a foreign language.
(or)
Good: To write in a foreign language is much easier than to speak in a foreign language.

Bad: She used to enjoy jogging, to ride horses and climbing mountains.

Good: She used to enjoy jogging, riding horses and climbing mountains.

Bad: You will need to come to the seminar with a new unlined notebook, two pencils and bring a compass.

Good: You will need to come to the seminar with a new unlined notebook, two pencils and a compass.

Bad: We learned how to find, interview and the hiring of new staff.

Good: We learned how to find, interview and hire new staff.

Bad: Company regulations require that you are carrying minimum medical insurance coverage, have regular health checkups, and will participate in the daily morning exercise program.

Good: Company regulations require that you carry minimum medical insurance coverage, have regular health checkups, and participate in the daily morning exercise program.

I. PRINCIPLE OF COHESIVENESS – B. SENTENCE LEVEL.
c. BE CONSISTENT

(9)   Keep Types of Words the Same.

When you refer to several items in a parallel structure, such as a list of items, keep the *types* of words in the list the same throughout. We will focus mainly on nouns here, but as we saw above, this rule to applies to the proper usage of verbs and other parts of speech.

Some nouns are derived from one common root word, and thus have more than one form as nouns. These words include "economy" ("economics"), "finance" ("financial") and "rationale" ("rationality"). A list of university academic degrees is illustrative of the kinds of differences that need to be dealt with. For example we have *economics, physics, linguistics, mathematics,* but instead of *politics,* the usual major is *political affairs*! And, what about *economics* (plural) but *high finance* and *business management* (singular)? For these, of course, you need to conform to context, and use the terms that are consistent and accepted within your field of use.

When you have a list of words, try to use words that all share the same endings, whenever possible, but more importantly, <u>use words that belong to the same class:</u> for example, *economic* is an <u>adjective</u> which refers to wealth or other aspects of life, *economics* is a <u>noun</u> which refers to the study or science of production, distribution and sales of goods, an *economist* (<u>noun</u>) is someone involved in such a study, *economical* is an <u>adjective</u> referring to limited expenses, *economically* is an <u>adverb</u> related to doing something at reasonable cost.

A more common error to be concerned about is the mixing of singular nouns with plural nouns, or, mixing count nouns (things that you can count, like "one pencil, two pencils") with mass nouns (things that you can only describe relatively, like "some bread" or "a lot of butter"). When you have parallel structures, such as lists, or when you are simply talking about two things, make sure that the parallel words are of the same form. If you do mix forms, make sure you qualify things clearly. Even when structures are not parallel, make sure you have the right form of the classifier matched with the nouns.

> Examples.

Bad: The previous *study* and *reports* all pointed out the need for a review of the safety provisions.

Good: The previous *studies* and *reports* all pointed out the need for a review of the safety provisions.

Bad: If you have any questions, feel free to consult *any of the staffs*.

Good: If you have any questions, feel free to consult *any member of the staff*.

Bad: I studied law, the economy and political affairs in college.

Good: I studied law, economics and political affairs in college.

Bad: You really can't compare *apples* and an *orange*.

Good: You really can't compare *apples* and *oranges*.

Bad: I'll have some coffee, pieces of toast and some scrambled eggs

Good: I'll have some coffee, toast and scrambled eggs.
(or)
Good: I'll have some coffee, scrambled eggs and two pieces of toast.

Bad: It is both practical and cheap to hire recent college graduates.

Good: It is both wise and cheap to hire recent college graduates.
(or)
Good: It is both practical and economical to hire recent college graduates.

I. PRINCIPLE OF COHESIVENESS – B. SENTENCE LEVEL.
c. BE CONSISTENT

(10)   Keep Degrees of Adjectives the Same.

Adjectives are words that are used to modify, clarify or condition nouns. There are three basic degrees of adjectives. There is the *positive* degree (adjectives such as *long, good* and *close*), the *comparative* degree (words such as *longer, better* and *closer*) and the *superlative* degree (words such as *longest, best* and *closest*). The general rule to follow here is when you have phrases or sentences in a parallel structure, you want to use the same degree for all of the adjectives in the parallel construction.

Positive degree adjectives refer to a quality of a noun, where no comparison to other nouns is implied. An example of positive degree adjectives:

"Someday I hope to buy not only a *new* car but a *fast* car."

Comparative degree adjectives are used in constructions that compare one thing to another. We have examples such as:

"Someday I'll buy not only a newer but a faster car than anything I've ever driven."

For *superlative* degree adjectives, there is also an element of comparison, as in the comparative adjectives, but in the case of superlatives, we are selecting out the ultimate item, the item that defines the extreme limit of whatever is being compared.

"This is the *fastest, quietest* car I have ever driven."

While it may be difficult to determine whether structures are parallel or not, the key point to remember here is that adjectives are in parallel construction when one or more of the adjectives directly modifies the same noun. When they are in these direct parallel structures, keep the degrees of the adjectives the same.

> Examples.

Bad: The telephone was the smallest and cheaper one at the store.

Good: The telephone was the smallest and cheapest one at the store.

Bad: She mentioned in the memo that the vases were both beautiful and cleaner.

Good: She mentioned in the memo that the vases were both beautiful and clean.

Bad: Not only is he smart, but he works fastest.

Good: Not only is he smart, but he works fast.

Bad: Their proposal was the most clearer and professional proposal of the day.

Good: Their proposal was the clearest and most professional proposal of the day.

Bad: The worse natural gas burning stove is better than the best coal burning stove.

Good: The worst natural gas burning stove is better than the best coal burning stove.

Bad: All of the new products were good, but the better one was the new EZ-1000 copier.

Good: All of the new products were good, but the best one was the new EZ-1000 copier.

I. PRINCIPLE OF COHESIVENESS – B. SENTENCE LEVEL.
d. AVOID DISTRACTIONS

(11)   Avoid Overly Simple Structures by Combining Simple Sentences.

Although a fundamental principle of Plain Written English is to minimize words in sentences, there is a limit to just how far we can go. If we simplify too much, then we run the risk of creating childlike, unsophisticated text. We need to seek a balance between the overly simple and the overly complex. Here, we consider the lower limits of what is acceptable, and provide simple guidelines for knowing when and how to combine simple sentences into slightly more complex, yet clear, professional writing forms.

In simplest terms, we can think of sentences as made up of one of two types of clauses, *independent* or *dependent*. *Independent* clauses are really just simple basic sentences that can stand alone, such as: "I ate dinner." or "The engineer spoke to us."

Dependent clauses, on the other hand, are sentences, or parts of sentences, that cannot exist by themselves. They must be added to independent clauses (usually with the help of subordinate conjunctions) in order to make good sentences. Here are some examples of dependent clauses: (bad) "Is wearing a blue jacket." or (bad) "I spoke with last week."

When we join dependent and independent clauses together, we get well-formed sentences: (good) "The engineer who is wearing a blue jacket spoke to us while we ate dinner." When we write a series of simple sentences made up of independent clauses, the effect is to leave the reader feeling spoken down to, or worse, our impression is that the writer can barely communicate above an elementary school level: "We started to eat dinner. The boss spoke to us. We finished dinner. The boss was still talking to us. The boss talked to us for nearly two hours." The easiest solution here is to simply employ coordinate conjunctions such as *and, then, or, while, after, before,* etc., to combine several of these independent clauses into a compound sentence: (good) "We ate while the boss spoke to us. The boss continued talking to us for nearly two hours." We can further improve upon this structure by deciding what the essential points are, and simply drop some things out: (good) "The boss spoke to us for nearly two hours, even during our dinner."

| Examples. |

Bad: I got up on time in the morning. I ate breakfast. I rode the subway to work. The subway was delayed. I got to work late.

Good: **Even though I got up on time today, the subway was delayed, so I was late to work.**

- -

Bad: Turn the computer on. Wait for the monitor to come on. Put the disk in the drive. Click on the disk icon.

Good: **First, turn the computer on, then after the monitor comes up put the disk in the drive and click on the icon when you see it.**

- -

Bad: Order three boxes of black ball-point pens. Order two cases of small tape dispensers. Order five hundred legal-sized notebooks.

Good: **Order three boxes of black ball-point pen, two cases of small tape dispensers and five hundred legal-sized notebooks.**

- -

Bad: Please call Ms. Lunquist. Make an appointment for me to see her. Ask her to look over the papers I sent her. The papers are on the new Applegate shopping mall.

Good: **Please call Ms. Lundquist and make an appointment for me to see her. Ask her to look over the papers I sent her on the new Applegate shopping mall.**

- -

Bad: Please fill out the pension plan form. Hand it to the personnel officer when you are done.

Good: **Please fill out the pension plan form and hand it to the personnel officer when you are done.**

- -

I. PRINCIPLE OF COHESIVENESS – B. SENTENCE LEVEL.
d. AVOID DISTRACTIONS

(12)   Avoid Perfect and Subjunctive Tenses.

We have already seen reasons to avoid complicated tenses in the discussion of basic sentence structure (Rule #5) and avoiding other complex verb structures such as the Passive, Causative and Conditionals (Rule #6). The Perfect and Subjunctive tenses, too, are generally to be avoided for the simple reason that they tend to confuse the issue being discussed, rather than clarify. What should we use instead? Just use the simple Past, Present and Future tenses whenever possible, with the progressive forms (*verb + ing* forms) as needed.

The Perfect tenses are tenses that use some form of the auxiliary "have" in the verb phrase. So, for example, we have the *present perfect tense* (I have eaten), the *present perfect progressive tense* (I have been eating), the *past perfect tense* (I had eaten) the *past perfect progressive tense* (I had been eating), and so forth. Rarely do you need to resort to these expressions, since the basic past, present and future tenses can cover virtually all situations more directly and more clearly.

The Subjunctive tense is even more complex, and therefore less useful, than the Perfect tense. The Subjunctive tense is made of the conditional "if" and a past tense statement *(If he were skinnier, he might run faster)*.

Sometimes the best solution to handling situations that might normally call for the perfective tense is to split the ideas up into two or three concrete ideas (they still may be contained within the structure of a single sentence, or broken into two or three different sentences). Although this suggestion seems to contradict Rule #11 *(add simple sentences together)*, this is not necessarily true, since our ultimate goal is precision and clarity, not confusion, which the Perfect and Subjunctive tenses tend to create. In some cases we do not need to abandon these tenses altogether, instead, just put them in the clear and more direct Subject-Verb-Object order.

| Examples. |

Bad: He had taken the test before I met him.

Good: I met him after he took the test.

Bad: Hisae will have taught the lesson before I get to the school.

Good: I will get to school after Hisae finishes teaching.

Bad: If he were more serious about his work he might get a promotion.

Good: He could get a promotion if he worked hard.

Bad: She would have no trouble getting her driver's license if she practiced more.

Good: She needs to practice more, then she should have no trouble getting her driver's license.
(or)
Good: She needs to practice more in order to get her driver's license.

Bad: For the last ten years, we have been ranking in the top five in sales in the region. In this memo I will be outlining steps to ensure that our success will continue for the next ten years as well.

Good: For the last ten years, we have ranked in the top five in sales in the region. In this memo I will outline steps to ensure that our success will continue for the next ten years as well.

Bad: If we were able to buy the land, we would have.

Good: We wanted to buy the land, but we were not able to.

I. PRINCIPLE OF COHESIVENESS – C. PARAGRAPH LEVEL.
a. CONFORM TO CONTEXT

(13)　　Know the Intended Audience, and Write to It.

One of the keys to good writing is to know who your audience is, and to write to their levels of understanding, interests and expectations. Before you begin, you need to consider who is going to read your text. Are you addressing just one specific individual, a group of specific individuals, or an unknown quantity of readers? The less you know about the audience, the more important it is for you to clarify new and unusual terms, and not to assume that everyone has the same understanding of (or interest in) the subject as yourself.

Whoever your audience is, it is generally appropriate to write in a natural unencumbered style, rather than in a formal pretentious manner. This does not mean that you should become too personal, colloquial or familiar. Think of the manner in which you would speak to these individuals if you were to address them in person, and try to replicate the same tone on paper. The tone should be friendly and understanding. It should appear that you are a person truly interested in the people you are writing to, that you value their attention and that you also are interested in their thoughts.

If it is a business letter, though, you probably don't want to dip below the semi-formal level unless the audience are members of your "inner circle" (close personal friends). This means that you should avoid most culturally loaded words and phrases, as well as slang and regional colloquialisms.

Finally, keep the text brief and to the point (ideas that are illustrated elsewhere in this text). No one wants to read a long and dull memo on a very simple and direct issue. Virtually everyone in the business world values time as highly as money, so it is best to write your ideas in simple direct prose, in a way that is immediately accessible to your particular audience, and contains only the things that they need to know, but conveyed in a way that is friendly and forthright, rather than stuffy and formal.

> Examples.

Bad: If I can be of any further assistance to you at this juncture, please don't hesitate getting in touch with me.

Good: **If I can be of any further help, please don't hesitate calling.**

Bad: In regards to your inquiry of May 21, I regret to inform you that we are unable to comply with your request.

Good: **Following up on your call of May 21, I am sorry to have to tell you that we can't do as you asked.**

Bad: You can be assured that your application is being given the utmost consideration at the highest levels of management, and that we will be in communication with you shortly as to the nature of our decision.

Good: **We are reviewing your application now, and we will inform you of our decision as soon as we can.**

Bad: I want you to pay close attention to my words, now, because I'll be after anyone who screws up.

Good: **Please pay careful attention to the suggestions I have listed in this memo.**

Bad: I would like to officially proclaim the eminent availability of our latest ink jet cartridge, the XP High Density Cartridge, now with nearly two-fold the printing integrity of our erstwhile low dispersion cartridges.

Good: **I would like to announce the release of our latest ink jet cartridge, the XP High Density Cartridge, now with nearly double the printing capacity of our former low density cartridges.**

I. PRINCIPLE OF COHESIVENESS – C. PARAGRAPH LEVEL.
a. CONFORM TO CONTEXT

(14)   Choose a Design and Stick to It.

Once you have determined your audience, you need to decide on an overall structure, and employ the structure consistently throughout the text. Try to imagine the kind of sequence, or narrative structure, that is most useful for the audience that you have identified.

There are various ways to order your thoughts, including *chronologically*, by *relative value* or *importance*, by *category*, and so forth. For all of these you should still use the basic sequence of starting with something that your audience recognizes, or understands, and work one step at a time from this common ground towards new and specific information. If there is controversy in store for your readers, lead them to it slowly, set them up, so that once you spring the surprise upon them, they are already well into the text. If, however, your writing is simply a summary of facts, such as an annual budget report, let the audience in on a bit of good news at the beginning, so they will be pleasantly disposed at reading the rest of the text. If there is bad news to be shared, again, let the audience in on it gradually, rather than dropping it on them all at once—let them warm up to the cause, and give them plenty of opportunities to see why such a situation occurred.

Before starting, whether your writing is a single page memo or a hundred page report, make a simple outline of the overall structure (in your head for the shorter notes, on paper for the longer ones). Guidelines for making outlines will be discussed in Rule #17, but for our purposes here, it is important to remember to <u>stick with whatever plan you choose</u>. Any deviations from an organized document usually look odd and out of place. Such digressions can be distracting and can in many situations weaken your arguments.

Remember, plan your message before you write it. Think about what you want to say, and what you want your audience to think. Organize your text so that your audience will *have* to come to the conclusions you want them to.

Examples.

Bad: Well, I guess I should give you a little background information.
Good: **I will begin by giving you some background information.**

Bad: I have now illustrated the seriousness of the problem, now I will tell you what I think might happen in the future, and then I'll tell you what I think caused the problem in the first place.
Good: **So far, I have discussed the seriousness of the problem and what I think caused it. Now I will tell you what I think might happen in the future.**

Bad: I have just reviewed the current sales figures for this quarter and last quarter, and the bad news is that our last quarter profits were much lower than expected. I'll tell you later what this means in terms of your jobs. The good news is that the current quarter's orders are coming at a rate much faster than expected.
Good: **I have just reviewed the current sales figures for this quarter and last quarter, and there is a mixed picture. On a positive note, our current orders are coming in much faster than we expected. On a less than positive note, however, last quarter's profits were lower than expected.**

Bad: We are committed to contributing to the public welfare in three basic areas; training, supplies and equipment. First, we will give free supplies to fund raising events, and second, we will allow free access to our printing equipment in support of the volunteer effort. Third, we will provide free technical training to volunteer organizations.
Good: **We are committed to contributing to the public welfare in three basic areas; training, supplies and equipment. First, we will provide free technical training to volunteer organizations. Second we will give free supplies to fund raising events, and third, we will allow free access to our printing equipment in support of the volunteer effort.**

I. PRINCIPLE OF COHESIVENESS - PARAGRAPH LEVEL.
a. CONFORM TO CONTEXT

(15)   Use the Correct Articles (a, an, the).

In general, the articles *a* or *an* are used before singular nouns that are unknown or unimportant. They are also used before nouns that are not specifically described. The basic rule: *Use a(n) to modify any one (object) of possibly many.* [Note: Use *an* before words starting with vowels or the silent 'h', use *a* elsewhere.]

The is used before nouns that have been mentioned before, are the topics under discussion, are specifically identified things, or are specific groups of identified things. For *an* and *a*, the important criteria is that the nouns which they modify are either unknown or unimportant, while the criteria for using *the* is that the noun it precedes is either known or important. The basic rule: *Use **the** to modify a specific one (object) of possibly many.*

There are three basic ways in which the noun may be made known (or important) to the audience. First, the information contained in the noun may be known to the audience by its having been mentioned at an earlier point in the communication.

  Sue: "I got a big box in the mail today."
  Sam: "Really? What was in *the* box?"

Secondly, a noun may be made known to the audience through explanatory information within the same sentence in which the "known" or "important" noun is contained.

  The box that Sue got in the mail today was large. (This implies that she received only one box.)

Finally, the third way in which a noun may be recognized by the listener is through observation and understanding of the situation it is used in—often common knowledge, or environmental facts, are relevant here.

  "Please turn off *the* air conditioner."

Finally, note that neither article is used for general statements, and the subject is usually plural in such statements. For example, "Using insecticides can be hazardous to your health." We would only say "Using *the* insecticides can be hazardous to your health," if we have already mentioned specifically *which* insecticides we were referring to. In general statements, however, when we have not mentioned specific items, articles are not used.

> Examples.

Bad: Please buy me the apple for lunch today.

Good: Please buy me an apple for lunch today.

Bad: Bob: "Could you fill in for Sam while he is on vacation?"
       Kenji: "Yes, of course. It would be a honor."

**Good: Bob: "Could you fill in for Sam while he is on vacation?"
       Kenji: "Yes, of course. It would be an honor."**

Bad: Have you ever seen a Tokyo Tower in Japan?

Good: Have you ever seen the Tokyo Tower in Japan?

Bad: For some people, flying in the airplane is a terrifying experience.

Good: For some people, flying in airplanes is a terrifying experience.

Bad: Sue: "I read the interesting book last week, you might like it."
       Sam: "Really? What is the book about?"

**Good: Sue: "I read an interesting book last week, you might like it."
       Sam: "Really? What is the book about?"**

Bad: I prefer to use the Mulligan computers over the ABM ones.

Good: I prefer to use Mulligan computers over ABM.

I. PRINCIPLE OF COHESIVENESS – C. PARAGRAPH LEVEL.
b. USE A LOGICAL ORDER

(16)   Organize Material Logically by Linking Paragraphs.

The typical paragraph begins with a topic statement, followed by supporting statements and ending with a brief summary or concluding statement, often something which sets the reader up for a slightly different tact to be taken in the next paragraph. In the following ten or so units, we will look at each of these different parts of the paragraph in greater detail, for our purposes here, however, we want to focus on the "global" properties of the paragraph as a unit, and the arrangement of these units into a text.

A text should be organized in a way that your readers will understand and expect. There are several different types of organizational styles available to you. If, for example, you are writing about stores located in different cities throughout the country, you might choose to discuss each store in *spatial order*, beginning with a store at one extreme (the furthest from where you are) and work slowly towards your present location by discussing the next nearest one (as if your order is one of links in a chain, where one link leads to another). Another common way to link paragraphs is to use *chronological* order. This is simply the order in terms of time in which events took place. In English, we usually start with the event that occurred furthest back in time, and work one event at a time towards the present. Still another common sequence is *cause and effect*, or *problem and solution*. In this sequence you begin by using one paragraph to discuss the problem, and a following paragraph to discuss what happened as a result, or what possible solutions are worth considering. Other popular organizational structures include *inductive* and *deductive* sequences. *Deductive* sequences are used when you arrange things in such a way as to basically tell your readers what to think, what they should conclude from the facts (that they should share or concur with your observations), while *inductive* sequences present the facts in such as way as to force your readers to decide for themselves what the solutions are. Finally, organizing your comments by their *order of importance* is a common linking sequence (usually from least to most).

Examples.

Bad: First, I will review the situation at our newest store, the outlet opened last February in Olympia, Washington. Next, I will discuss the problems concerning the three stores in the Washington D.C. area, which are probably the most important concerns facing us now. Then, I will look at the complaints that have come up over our plans to expand the mid-west warehouse in Kansas City, which I think is quite a minor issue.

Good: **First, I will address the complaints that have come up over our plans to expand the mid-west warehouse in Kansas City, which I think is quite a minor issue. Next, I will review the situation at our newest store, the outlet opened last February in Olympia, Washington. Finally, I will discuss the problems concerning the three stores in the Washington D.C. area, which are probably the most important concerns facing us now.**

Bad: The problems we are facing today include low employee morale, poor working conditions and limited production output. In the following discussion, I will offer suggestions for improving these conditions (....). As you know, when the owner passed away last Fall, the company has been managed by a temporary supervisory team, brought in from the outside. This situation (....) has clearly caused various problems here at the company.

Good: **As you know, when the owner passed away last Fall, the company has been managed by a temporary supervisory team, brought in from the outside. This situation (....) has clearly caused various problems here at the company.**
The problems we are facing today include low employee morale, poor working conditions and limited production output. In the following discussion, I will offer suggestions for improving these conditions (....).

I. PRINCIPLE OF COHESIVENESS – C. PARAGRAPH LEVEL.
b. USE A LOGICAL ORDER

(17) <u>Begin a Paragraph with a Good Topic Sentence.</u>

The paragraph is a unit that is suitable for virtually any kind of text, and has a certain loosely defined structure of its own. In general, we begin a paragraph with a topic sentence, which introduces the main subject and the point of view, or focus, and then we offer supporting statements before concluding with a brief summary statement. If the paragraph is the first one in the text, it is used to set the tone for the rest of your discussion, so make sure the statement is clear, precise, and tells the audience exactly what you are going to be talking about in the discussion. The topic statements of the paragraphs which follow the first paragraph should be linked to the preceding paragraphs. Efforts should be made to make the transition a smooth one from one paragraph to another.

If your paragraph is going to add further support to the points raised in the preceding paragraph, tell your readers as much. Here, we can use key words and phrases such as "*again,*" "*secondly,*" "*next,*" "*If we took this one step further,*" "*In addition to the points raised above,*" and so forth.

If your discussion is going to take a turn in a different direction, tell your audience by using terms such as "*despite the evidence discussed above,*" "*alternatively,*" "*if, on the other hand,*" and so forth. Sometimes the change in direction, from one paragraph to another, is great enough to warrant a complete *paragraph of transition,* so that the reader can make the jump from one idea to the other easily.

Overall, a paragraph is a unit composed of sentences (rarely does one sentence make a paragraph). A single paragraph can be thought of as a single thought, or idea. It can be a brief description of an event, a planned action, a single product or some other simple issue. It needs to hold together as an independent unit, and should not be too brief nor too long. Short paragraphs usually seem shallow or incomplete, while overly long paragraphs seem dense and cumbersome. For very long paragraphs, it is usually best to break them into smaller less formidable paragraphs. Usually a good length for a paragraph is between four and eight sentences long.

| Examples. |

Bad: I will review the factors that have contributed most significantly to the trade imbalance. The biggest problem facing U.S.-Japanese relations is the budget deficit. There are many factors which have led to the deficit, many of which cannot be attributed to any one country in particular.

Good: **The biggest problem facing U.S.-Japanese relations is the budget deficit. There are many factors which have led to the deficit, many of which cannot be attributed to any one country in particular. In the following discussion, I will review the factors that have contributed most significantly to the trade imbalance.**

Bad: We will be able to consider other issues, such as differences in the service sector, differences in quality control, and differences in product design only after we have a basic understanding of each country's distribution system. First of all, we must look at the issue of product distribution, and how the methods of distribution differ from one country to the other.

Good: **First of all, we must look at the issue of product distribution, and how the methods of distribution differ from one country to the other. Only after we have a basic understanding of each country's distribution system we will then be able to consider other issues, such as differences in the service sector, differences in quality control, and differences in product design.**

I. PRINCIPLE OF COHESIVENESS – C. PARAGRAPH LEVEL.
b. USE A LOGICAL ORDER

(18)   Using Facts and Statistics in Supporting Statements.

After you have written your topic statement, you then need to support this statement in one of several ways. In this section, we will focus on using facts and statistics to support our opening statement. Supporting statements develop points raised in the topic statement. They serve to provide concrete examples, clear illustrations, vivid details and the like.

Facts are used to support your statements when you think that your readers may not believe your claims, be aware of the issues or understand the true causes of the problems. Facts should be attributed to sources other than "*they say,*" or "*it has been claimed.*" Generally, you would state facts using the following phrases "*according to (someone's name, or a report),*" "*Mr. (someone's name) noted in the January 2012 edition of...*" Usually, when you use facts in formal business text such as reports, you must also say where you got the facts from. In less formal writings, such as in office memos, it may not be necessary to note the sources, especially if you are certain your audience is already aware of these facts. Nevertheless, *be sure that you have stated the facts correctly*, and in the context in which they were intended. Misrepresented facts will ultimately weaken your arguments, rather than strengthen them.

Similarly, statistics can be used to support your topic sentence. Statistics are essentially facts that are organized into categories, and through interpretation, provide information that can be used for comparison and contrast. For statistics, as with facts, it is important to document the source of the figures that you are citing. You should be convinced that the statistics *and the interpretations* are accurate, and truly do support your claims. This is only possible by carefully reading the original report in which the statistics were developed. If you simply look at the statistics without a careful study of where they came from, or how meticulously they were developed, you are leaving your own arguments vulnerable to those readers who may have an even better understanding of the statistics that you have cited.

> Examples.

Bad: I have heard that ABM is planning on releasing two new lap top computers by the end of the year.

Good: **ABM is planning on releasing two new lap top computers by the end of the year.**

Bad: They say that we need to cut down on production costs by ten percent.

Good: **The head office says that we need to cut down on production costs by ten percent.**

Bad: Japan suffers a major trade imbalance not only with the U.S., but also with the European Community.

Good: **The 2012 U.S. Department of Commerce Annual Report shows that Japan suffers a major trade imbalance not only with the U.S., but also with the European Community.**

Bad: According to my uncle, who lives in Minneapolis, the rate of bank failures in Minnesota is very high.

Good: **According to the Minnesota Association of Banking and Investment Institutions, the rate of bank failures in Minnesota is very high.**

Bad: There are several good arguments against the use of lead in making food containers.

Good: **There are several good arguments against the use of lead in making food containers, including those made by the U.S. Surgeon General.**

I. PRINCIPLE OF COHESIVENESS – C. PARAGRAPH LEVEL.
b. USE A LOGICAL ORDER

(19) <u>Using Examples and Lists as Supporting Statements.</u>

When we have several points that all relate to, or support, a topic statement, we may wish to list these points. Lists can be organized *chronologically* (in time: first, second, third...), *spatially* (by location: near, nearer, nearest), *alphabetically* (apples, bananas, cherries...), in *order of importance* (cost, size, appearance) or *numerically* (1st, 2nd, 3rd).

When using *time* to order a sequence, it is best to begin with what occurred furthest back in time, and work towards the present.

For *spatial* sequences, it is best to start with the familiar (some location everyone immediately recognizes) and work towards the unfamiliar. Or, if everyone knows all of the locations from the onset, then it is best simply to use the "chain link" sequence, starting from one end of the chain or the other.

For *alphabetical* sequences, it is natural to start with the first letter of the alphabet (*a*) and work towards the last (*z*).

When ordering things in a list by *importance*, we usually start with the least important, or lowest priority, and work towards the highest.

For *numerical* sequences, it usually preferred to start with the lowest figures first, and work on up to the highest figures. In some countries, there are some differences. For example, it is common to see bargain sales being advertised in foreign stores with savings of 80% - 50% off, or 30% - 10% off. In the U.S., however, you would never see this sequence. Instead, you would see savings advertised as 50% - 80% off, or 10% - 30% off (low to high, rather than high to low).

Whichever order you choose when you are listing a series of similar examples, it is important to not <u>mix</u> different orders. You might ask when is a list a list, or when is a group of items just a group? Generally, if you have just two or three items, such as city names, then any order will do (i.e., this is a group, not a list). However, when you have four, five or more similar examples, then it is best to try to adopt one of the listing sequences discussed here.

> Examples.

Bad: We have many outlets between Sapporo and Fukuoka. These include ones in Osaka, Tokyo, Nagoya, Sendai and Hiroshima.

Good: **We have many outlets between Sapporo and Fukuoka. These include ones in Sendai, Tokyo, Nagoya, Osaka and Hiroshima.**

Bad: Our wholesale distribution center is open on Thursdays until 6 PM, Tuesdays until 8 PM and Saturdays until 6 PM.

Good: **Our wholesale distribution center is open on Tuesdays until 8 PM, Thursdays until 6 PM and Saturdays until 6 PM.**

Bad: Between ninety and eighty percent of all of our employees have an advanced college degree.

Good: **Between eighty and ninety percent of all of our employees have an advanced college degree.**

Bad: Nagoya is our smallest producer, Tokyo is our largest producer which is followed by Osaka.

Good: **Tokyo is our largest producer, followed by Osaka, then Nagoya.**

Bad: We would like to have current prices for several types of fruit, including; figs, papayas, apples, bananas, apples, melons and grapes.

Good: **We would like to have current prices for several types of fruit, including; apples, bananas, figs, grapes, melons and papayas.**

I. PRINCIPLE OF COHESIVENESS – C. PARAGRAPH LEVEL.
b. USE A LOGICAL ORDER

(20)   <u>Using Opinions as Supporting Statements.</u>

Another way to support a topic sentence is to use an opinion, either your own, or someone else's. In general, another person's opinion carries more weight than your own, since your whole text is essentially already telling us what you believe. In other words, if you can find others who believe the same things that you claim, then you have additional external support for your statement. Like facts and statistics (see Rule #18, above), it is usually necessary to tell the audience who made these claims. Further, since there are usually no facts or statistics involved in opinions, it is also necessary to tell the reader why the person whose opinions you have cited should be believed. Why should this person be regarded as an authority on the issue?

This is a hole into which many journalists fall into. Whenever a calamity strikes, if there are known "personalities" that are affected, they are often treated as if they are experts on the situation, where instead, they may have no knowledge, background or understanding that qualifies their opinions as useful. So, it is important to determine just how much credence the person has that you are citing. Does your audience know this person, or at least recognize the value of his credentials? If not, if you cite someone no one knows, from a group no one has ever heard of, it may in fact weaken your arguments, rather than support them. The impression is that you can't find anyone recognizable to support your statements, and that you pulled in an irrelevant "expert" that in fact carries no weight).

Remember that opinions are much less persuasive than facts and statistics. They are best used when there is clear evidence supporting the conclusions, yet not enough to be able to attribute the evidence to any one person or thing. When there is strong reason to believe these opinions, then go ahead and use them, but make sure you are clear to the audience that these claims are indeed opinions, and that you do not misrepresent them as facts.

> Examples.

Bad: The head of the engineering department said that he thought the change in the dollar and yen exchange rate wouldn't be a major problem.

Good: The chief economist in the finance ministry said that he thought the change in the dollar and yen exchange rate wouldn't be a major problem.

Bad: I personally believe, and I know of others who support me on this, that our production rate is working below maximum capacity at the moment.

Good: Several members of the senior staff believe that our production rate is working below maximum capacity at the moment.

Bad: I learned firsthand from an expert that mercury batteries are quite toxic and will no longer be made.

Good: I learned firsthand from an engineer at the Duracell® battery company that mercury batteries are quite toxic and will no longer be made.

Bad: According to a few doctors I talked to, drinking moderate amounts of beer is not necessarily harmful to your body.

Good: According to American Medical Association, drinking moderate amounts of beer is not necessarily harmful to your body.

Bad: The world record for throwing something by hand is more than 1,000 feet.

Good: The world record for throwing something by hand is more than 1,000 feet, according to the Guinness Book of Records.

I. PRINCIPLE OF COHESIVENESS – C. PARAGRAPH LEVEL.
b. USE A LOGICAL ORDER

(21)   Making Statements of Comparison and Contrast.

When we **compare** two or more items together, we are generally looking for both areas that are similar amongst the items being compared, and also what qualities or features distinguish each item from the others. On the other hand, when we **contrast** two or more things, we are primarily concerned only with the differences that distinguish one item from the others. Both comparison and contrast are useful when two or more facts are recognized to be relevant to a topic, but where one supports the claim and the other weakens the claim. Alternatively, comparison can simply be used to discuss the relative advantages or disadvantages that one thing has over another. We have already discussed the three degrees of comparison at the word level (see Rule #10), here we will focus on comparison and contrast at the paragraph level.

Essentially, at this level of writing, we use comparison and contrast to focus, or emphasize, key features of an idea, a person, a place or a thing. It is clearest to simply compare and contrast only two items at once, rather than considering several items simultaneously. For example, in English there is the expression *You can't compare apples to oranges,* which, if we added a third item to the list, becomes quite unclear: *You can't compare apples to oranges and (or) bananas.* So, if at all possible, make your comparisons one-to-one, rather than one-to-many. If you have several items that must be considered, then do so one at a time or simply summarize your findings in a group statement: *Apples sell better year round than any other fruit (rather than Apples sell better than oranges and bananas all year round).*

Basically, then, comparison and contrast is used to emphasize, or focus, on something that we think supports our topic statement. Key expressions for comparison include, *the same as, different from, as....as, more...than,* and the other expressions covered in Rule #10, above. Sometimes, or course, our conclusion is that there are no differences between two alternatives, which can be important in its own right.

> Examples.

Bad: The problems with selling automobiles are not the same with selling food products.

Good: **The problems with selling automobiles are not the same as with selling food products.**

Bad: Foreign rice is harder to clean and cook from domestic rice.

Good: **Foreign rice is harder to clean and cook than domestic rice.**

Bad: A key difference with the new super microchips and the older ones is in processing speed. The super chips outperform the older ones by more than a margin of two to one.

Good: **A key difference between the new super microchips and the older ones is in processing speed. The super chips outperform the older ones by more than a margin of two to one.**

Bad: Though domestic beef costs as much of twice the cost of imported rice, customers still prefer to buy domestic beef.

Good: **Though domestic beef costs as much as twice the cost of imported rice, customers still prefer to buy domestic beef.**

Bad: Work conditions in the city are different to work conditions in the country.

Good: **Work conditions in the city are different from work conditions in the country.**

I. PRINCIPLE OF COHESIVENESS – C. PARAGRAPH LEVEL.
b. USE A LOGICAL ORDER

(22) Using the Cause and Effect Sequence.

The sequence of *cause* and *effect* (and also, *problem* and *solution*) can be used both within a paragraph and from one paragraph to another (see Rule #16, above). Here, we will focus on using cause and effect within a paragraph. Basically this is a sequence which requires two different situations, a *before* (cause) and an *after* (effect) situation.

Usually the *before*, or *cause*, statement can be a statement of fact, such as:

The company suffered major losses last year.

This statement may be followed by a few sentences that add further details, or depth, to the topic statement, such as:

We needed to sell 12 tons of rice to break even, but, due to the poor harvest we in fact only sold 8 tons.

After these additional details, we are ready for the transition to the *after* or *effect* part of the paragraph. This is signaled by using transition words and phrases such as *accordingly, as a result, subsequently, for these reasons, therefore, due to, in view of,* and *so*. Continuing our example here, then, we might have:

As a result, we are unable to buy the new equipment this year as planned.

The cause and effect sequence can be used for a variety of situations, such as setting up a problem that requires a solution, illustrating an unfortunate situation, highlighting a successful approach to handling a troublesome issue, and so forth. The key point here is that it is best to use the logical order of stating the cause *first*, and *then* what the *consequences* were, rather than going in the reverse order.

> Examples.

Bad: We will be considering other distribution companies when the current contract expires this January. During the last year, the distribution company raised its prices three times, so that we are now paying more for everything than ever before. Last year we signed a contract with a new distribution company, and because of the contract, we have been obligated to purchase all of our office supplies through them.

Good: **Last year we signed a contract with a new distribution company, and because of the contract, we are obligated to purchase all of our office supplies through them. During the year, the distribution company raised its prices three times, so that we are now paying more for everything than ever before. As a result, we will be considering other distribution companies when the current contract expires this January.**

Bad: You are welcome to have any position that is vacant at a salary level equal to your old job. Unfortunately, it is not clear at the moment just what vacancies we might have. During your absence, we hired a temporary replacement to take over your job while you were out. The new employee has been doing well in your old position, so we would like her to stay in this job.

Good: **During your absence, we hired a temporary replacement to take over your job while you were out. The new employee has been doing well in your old position, so we would like her to stay in this job. As for you, you are welcome to have any position that is vacant at a salary level equal to your old job. Unfortunately, it is not clear at the moment just what vacancies we might have.**

I. PRINCIPLE OF COHESIVENESS – C. PARAGRAPH LEVEL.
b. USE A LOGICAL ORDER

(23)   Making Clear Transitions within a Paragraph.

In the last several sections we have been looking at the structure of a paragraph. In this section we continue on the theme of moving from one point to another within a single paragraph, something that we touched on in the last section. Why do we need a transition within a paragraph, since a paragraph is supposed to contain a single idea? As we saw in the last section, on cause and effect, the idea may be fairly complex, and may require movement from one idea to another. This happens of course from one paragraph to another, but it can happen just as easily within a paragraph. As a result, many of the transition elements that can take us from one paragraph to another paragraph can also be used to take us from one sentence to another. Besides sequences such as cause and effect, we have sequences that *reinforce* a point, *contradict* a point, or *clarify* a point.

When we have a statement that *reinforces* an earlier statement (usually the topic statement), we need to link this supporting statement to the preceding one with appropriate words of transition. These words include: *furthermore, in addition, indeed* and *moreover*.
For example:
> *The weather is expected to continue to be cool throughout the summer.*
> *In addition, higher amounts of rain are predicted.*

When we wish to *contradict* or *refute* a preceding statement, we use transition words such as *however, nevertheless, on the contrary, on the other hand,* and *still*.
> *The weather is expected to continue to be cool throughout the summer.*
> *Still, I think we will meet our production goals.*

When we wish to *clarify* a preceding statement, so that it is clear perfectly what we mean by it, we use transition words such as *namely, for instance, to illustrate, in other words, that is, to clarify* and *to be more specific*.
> *The weather is expected to continue to be cool throughout the summer.*
> *To be more specific, the temperatures should average 4 or 5 degrees less than last year.*

| Examples. |

Bad: The company enjoyed a higher profit because of the strengthened dollar. A difficult lawsuit was settled at no cost to the company when it was found to have no liabilities in the case.

Good: The company enjoyed a higher profit because of the strengthened dollar. In addition, a difficult lawsuit was settled at no cost to the company when it was found to have no liabilities in the case.

Bad: We have lost three employees to our rival across town. I don't think there should be any problem meeting the deadline on your rush order.

Good: We have lost three employees to our rival across town. Still, I don't think there should be any problem meeting the deadline on your rush order.

Bad: There are several areas that still need improvement before we will be able to improve our production. We need to find ways to use more of our by-products, so that we can cut down on disposal costs.

Good: There are several areas that still need improvement before we will be able to improve our production. To be more specific, we need to find ways to use more of our by-products, so that we can cut down on disposal costs.

Bad: Due to the continuing recession, we have had to cut back on the number of new employees we will be able to hire this spring. This trend will continue on into the next year, likely.

Good: Due to the continuing recession, we have had to cut back on the number of new employees we will be able to hire this spring. Also, it is likely that this trend will continue on into the next year.

I. PRINCIPLE OF COHESIVENESS – C. PARAGRAPH LEVEL.
b. USE A LOGICAL ORDER

(24)   Summarizing your Points.

Summarization is used both at the end of a paragraph and at the end of the text. A summary should review the key issues or points of the discussion. It should highlight only the most pertinent information that you have discussed, and should not contain any new points. It should be short, compact and to the point, not burdened with unnecessary details, irrelevant issues, or useless information.

At the paragraph level this can be done in a single sentence, or perhaps two. It need not summarize everything that preceded it, but rather, simply tie things together so that the paragraph can stand alone as a unit, and allow the reader to move on to the next paragraph with a clear idea of what she has just read. Rarely is it necessary to repeat points or restate facts at the paragraph level, instead, simply end (the paragraph) with a statement that prepares the reader to move on to the next point.

At the conclusion of the text, on the other hand, it is sometimes useful to repeat a point, or restate a key fact, so that the audience is once again reminded of the information that you consider important. Remember, though, it is distracting to have every point repeated, so be selective, and focus on key issues. Further, don't assume that your audience has necessarily accepted your claims completely. Treat issues from other perspectives, ones that they might likely embrace, and show how your arguments work from these alternative perspectives as well. Finally, if there is action to be taken as a result of your discussion, tell the audience specifically what action is required, how to go about doing it, and what the goals are, setting any other parameters that you feel necessary (such as establishing time limits, quality controls, etc.).

Useful words for completing a list of ideas, a sequence of points, or the like (within a paragraph, or at the end of a series of paragraphs) include: *last, lastly, finally* and *the final point*. Key words to use in summarizing your text at the end of the document include: *to conclude, to summarize, in summary, in conclusion, to close, in closing, in brief* and *in short*.

> Examples.

Bad: In the next several months, we will be doing a complete review of our plant facilities. We will look at the printing shop. After the spring meeting is over, we will take a look at the planning office and make an analysis of the construction factory. We will take on the large task of investigating the storage and distribution center.

Good: **In the next several months, we will be doing a complete review of our plant facilities. We will begin with a look at the printing shop. Then, after the spring meeting is over, we will take a look at the planning office followed by an analysis of the construction factory. Finally we will conclude by taking on the large task of investigating the storage and distribution center.**

Bad: It is essential that we pay attention to the recent concern in protecting the environment. It is clear that we have to expand our production capacity, while at the same time, make better use of existing resources. We do have a building in the downtown Philadelphia area that is presently being utilized. I think we should simply refurbish the Philadelphia facility.

Good: **To summarize, I'd like to emphasize a few of the key points that I have brought out here. First, it is essential that we pay attention to the recent concern in protecting the environment. Second, it is clear that we have to expand our production capacity, while at the same time, make better use of existing resources. Third, we do have a building in the downtown Philadelphia area that is presently being utilized. Lastly, because of these facts it is my position that we can expand our capacity without harming the environment by simply refurbishing the Philadelphia facility.**

I. PRINCIPLE OF COHESIVENESS – C. PARAGRAPH LEVEL.
b. USE A LOGICAL ORDER

(25)   Emphasizing your Points.

If you have points that you want to emphasize, it is best to include these points either in the first sentence of a paragraph, in topic position, or in the last sentence of a paragraph, in summary position. These two positions stand out structurally as the two most important sentences in a paragraph, and, if used to stress important ideas, do not detract from the overall structure of the paragraph. If, on the other hand, the important ideas you wish to emphasize are placed amongst supporting statements within the paragraph, then the balance of the paragraph will be thrown off, with important ideas sitting next to relatively unimportant supporting details. An important idea placed within the paragraph requires unnecessary and awkward transitions from sentence to sentence.

When you are choosing what to highlight, or to emphasize, choose the things that your audience will likely to respond to. What benefit is there for the reader personally? State how things will improve for the readers specifically, whenever possible. Try to avoid simply listing new features, or characteristics, that are included in your discussion. Instead, emphasize how these features will make a positive impact, in some form or another, on the lives of your readers. For example, if you have a product such as a portable computer that weighs significantly less than its predecessors, don't simply dwell on the facts (it weighs just 12 ounces), but focus on how much easier it will be for your clients to carry this portable computer around with them, and that they may even have room to carry their lunch as well.

Some key words and expressions to use when you wish to place an emphasis on an idea include: *above all, notably, by all means, absolutely, most of all, furthermore, significantly, the most significant, truly, positively, absolutely, the most* and *extremely.*

> Examples.

Bad: There are many issues that confront us today, and having a good product to sell is the most important goal for us.

Good: There are many issues that confront us today, but above all else, having a good product to sell is the most important goal for us.

Bad: The quality inspectors pointed out several minor things that we need to clean up. They said that we need to replace all of the refrigerator thermostats, we need to find a better way to dispose of non-burnable garbage, and a few other things. They said nothing about our food preparation standards, which is what we worked hard on to improve. Congratulations to all of you who helped to correct this problem.

Good: The quality inspectors pointed out several minor things that we need to clean up. Specifically, they said that we need to replace all of the refrigerator thermostats, we need to find a better way to dispose of non-burnable garbage, and a few other things. Notably, though, they said nothing about our food preparation standards, which is what we worked hard on to improve. Congratulations to all of you who helped to correct this problem.

Bad: As you consider our offer, feel free to discuss this with any of our employees, we want you to be certain that you are willing to take the assignment.

Good: As you consider our offer, by all means feel free to discuss this with any of our employees, we want you to be absolutely certain that you are willing to take the assignment.

Bad: The new model is not only more efficient, but, it is cheaper.

Good: The new model is not only more efficient, but significantly, it is cheaper.

I. PRINCIPLE OF COHESIVENESS – C. PARAGRAPH LEVEL.
c. BE CONSISTENT

(26)   Avoid Shifts in Person.

In this section, we build and expand upon the idea of using first person singular (see rule #4). First, *it is always best to maintain the same person throughout the same text.* So, if you begin with first person singular, as recommended, try to use this perspective throughout your entire text. However, in some cases you may feel a need to put some distance between you, the writer, and the subject, or similarly, between the intended audience and the subject. In such situations, it is sometimes useful to use the indeterminate "one(s)," or even "you," instead of "I." When using these other persons in your statements, though, the same rule applies, namely, use the same person throughout the relevant area of the text.

Bad: *One* must be ready to suffer the consequences of *their* actions.
Bad: *One* must be ready to suffer the consequences of *his* actions.
Good: *One* must be ready to suffer the consequences of *one's* actions.

In the first two examples, above, it is incorrect to replace the second subject reference (one's) with a different person (*his, your, their,* etc.), since this violates the rule of consistency of subject reference. Similarly, if you do choose to use the first person singular writing perspective, it is best not to mix singular and plural references (*I* and *we*), at least not *within* a paragraph.

Bad: *I* will discuss this later when *we* go over your employment record.
Good: *We* will discuss this later when *we* go over your employment record.
        (or)
Good: *I* will discuss this later when *I* go over your employment record.

There are times when this rule is violated within a paragraph, but for our purposes of Plain Written English, it is best simply to avoid such violations, and stick to first person singular whenever possible for your own ideas, and <u>one</u> other detached form (such as *one*, or *you*), and not a mixture of different forms. Remember, though, that using the detached forms tend to formalize your writing, depersonalize your ideas, and put a distance between you and your audience, and should only be used when such distance is necessary.

> Examples.

Bad: Whether one prefers the total control of manual operation or the simplicity of use of the automatic mode depends on what you are used to.
Good: **Whether you prefer the total control of manual operation or the simplicity of use of the automatic mode depends on what you are used to.**
(or)
Good: **Whether one prefers the total control of manual operation or the simplicity of use of the automatic mode depends on what one is used to.**

Bad: After being out on sick leave for more than three days, one needs to bring a note signed by your doctor describing one's reason for being out.
Good: **After being out on sick leave for more than three days, you need to bring a note signed by your doctor describing your reason for being out.**

Bad: I would like to arrange a meeting for everyone when we have received all of the final changes to the contract bids.
Good: **I would like to arrange a meeting for everyone when I have received all of the final changes to the contract bids.**

Bad: One is expected to report any systems errors to the controls officer as soon as they have been detected.
Good: **You are expected to report any systems errors to the controls officer as soon as they have been detected.**

Bad: As part of the management team, I can safely say that they are in favor of your promotion.
Good: **As part of the management team, I can safely say that we are in favor of your promotion.**

I. PRINCIPLE OF COHESIVENESS – C. PARAGRAPH LEVEL.
c. BE CONSISTENT

(27) <u>Avoid Shifts in Number.</u>

In this section, we focus on the *number* (*singular* or *plural*) of subjects and objects. Just as in the last section, whenever possible, we want to avoid the mixing of forms. In this case, then, we want to avoid referring to subjects and objects as singular in one instance and plural in another, especially if the subject (or object) refers to the same group of items. It is probably best to begin with an illustration of mixed number (a violation of Plain Written English) subjects.

Bad: *He* should try to work out the difficulties by *themselves*.
Good: ***They*** **should try to work out the difficulties by *themselves*.**
(or)
Good: ***He*** **should try to work out the difficulties by *himself*.**

In the example, above, we have *he* and *themselves* referring to the same individual(s). Since the reference is unclear (we don't know really if there are several people involved), the sentence is clearly confusing. If the detached subject reference is employed (*one*) there is even greater likelihood of error:

Bad: *One* should try to work out *their* own difficulties.
Good: ***One*** **should try to work out *one's* own difficulties.**
(or)
Good: ***They*** **should try to work out *their* own difficulties.**

Sometimes the confusion about number references in a sentence is brought about by other phrases in the sentence that tend to mask, or hide, the connection between the subject and its reference. In these situations, it is advisable to simply look past these phrases, and make sure the subjects agree.

Bad: Please tell Mr. Johnson to send the copies over right away, and tell them to send the originals too.
Good: **Please tell Mr. Johnson to send the copies over right away, and tell him to send the originals too.**

When in doubt about subject references, just trim the sentence back to the basic sequence of SVO and determine from the basic sentence what needs to agree with what.

> Examples.

Bad: The bank will refund your money within six weeks of receipt of your inquiry, if there are any funds remaining in your account. The delay is because they must be certain that there are no outstanding debts.

Good: **The bank will refund your money within six weeks of receipt of your inquiry, if there are any funds remaining in your account. The delay is because the bank must be certain that there are no outstanding debts.**

Bad: Mr. Morita at the Bank of Seattle said that they would be happy to have his bank be a sponsor in the charity fund-raiser.

Good: **Mr. Morita at the Bank of Seattle said that he would be happy to have his bank be a sponsor in the charity fund-raiser.**

Bad: The section chief, as a member of the management team, always tries to work things out by themselves.

Good: **The section chief, as a member of the management team, always tries to work things out by himself.**

Bad: Mr. Grand asked that after the tests had been made, the questionnaires were to be filled out and returned to him as soon as possible. They should be sent to them by express mail.

Good: **Mr. Grand asked that after the tests had been made, the questionnaires were to be filled out and returned to him as soon as possible. The questionnaires should be sent to him by express mail.**

I. PRINCIPLE OF COHESIVENESS – C. PARAGRAPH LEVEL.
c. BE CONSISTENT

(28)   Avoid Shifts in Voice.

Voice refers to whether something is said in the basic SVO order (i.e. *active voice*), or if the order is reversed to an OVS sequence (i.e. *passive voice*). We have already introduced several rules that should help to avoid a shift in voice from arising (Rules #4, 5, 6), but there will be situations where it is necessary to use the Passive voice. The rule here is to avoid shifting from active to passive voice (or vice versa) within the same paragraph, and even more importantly, from shifting within the same sentence. Once you have determined the best voice to use to communicate your idea, stick to it throughout that portion of the text that is relevant. The following are examples of the right way and the wrong way to handle voice in sentences.

Bad: The man who talked to Bill *has been leaving*.
Good: The man who talked to Bill *left*.

- -

Bad: As I walked into the room, the 5 o'clock whistle *was being heard* by the men.
Good: As I walked into the room, the 5 o'clock whistle blew.

Passive structures are sentences that contain the *be* verb and a *past participle* form of a verb (these part participle forms include *seen, heard, taken, written, eaten*, etc.—often called the *-en* forms of verbs). As stated before, these forms require the natural SVO sentence order to be reversed, and additional words to be added to the sentences, so whenever possible, it is best to simply avoid Passives altogether, and keep verbs in their *active* forms. By keeping things in the *active*, you don't have to worry about shifts in voice, or sentence order problems. So, when possible, use *I see it* (instead of *It is seen by me), *She drives a taxi* (instead of **A taxi is driven by her*), and *The company bought the cheaper brand* (instead of **A cheaper brand was bought by the company*), and so forth.

> Examples.

Bad: Everyone needs to get a copy of the environmental impact report. They are supposed to have been read the report before the next meeting.

Good: Everyone needs to get a copy of the environmental impact report. They are expected to read the report before the next meeting.

Bad: As we get near the end of the year, a slowdown in production is being seen by us and our competitors. We need to watch our spending carefully over the next several weeks, so that cash reserves be not all used up.

Good: As we get near the end of the year, we, as well as our competitors, are seeing a slowdown in production. We need to watch our spending carefully over the next several weeks, so that we do not use up all of our cash reserves.

Bad: I am referring to the copier that is being used by your staff. It is not being found to be in very good operating condition, especially when we try to print color artwork.

Good: I am referring to the copier that your staff is using. It is not in very good operating condition, especially when we try to print color artwork.

Bad: Since the work will done in an area where there are no paved roads, our old trucks will be used instead of the ones we just got in last week.

Good: Since the work will be done in an area where there are no paved roads, we will use our old trucks instead of the ones we just got in last week.

- 67 -

I. PRINCIPLE OF COHESIVENESS – C. PARAGRAPH LEVEL.
c. BE CONSISTENT

(29)   Avoid Shifts in Tense.

We have already determined that the present tense is preferred in business writing (see rule #4). However, sometimes it is necessary to discuss events that took place in the past, or will take place in the future, as well as situations where one thing occurred before, or after, another. For these situations, it is best to stay with one form of the past tense, or one form of the future, throughout the paragraph, and certainly within a single sentence. Even when describing events chronologically, stick to one tense, rather than mixing tenses.

The future tense has several different forms, including *I will eat (will + verb)*, *I will be eating (will be verb-ing)* and, *I am about to eat (to + verb)*. Our rule here, *Avoid Shifts in Tense*, suggests that combining forms, such as combining the *will + verb* form and the *will be verb-ing* form, within a single idea, is not permissible.

Bad: I *will eat* dinner with the boss and *will be drinking* champagne, too.
Good: I *will eat* dinner with the boss and *will drink* champagne, too.

Similarly, there are several forms available for past tense expressions. These include *I ate, I was eating, I had eaten, I have eaten, I have been eating* and *I had been eating*. Here too, we want to avoid mixing tenses.

Bad: I *ate* dinner with the boss and *was drinking* champagne, too.
Good: I *ate* dinner with the boss and *drank* champagne, too.

There are situations where we want to mention events in order of occurrence, where some things are clearly past events, others present, and still possibly others future expectations. In these situations, it is of course acceptable to employ more than one tense. In chronologically ordered sequences, though, stick to one *type* of tense progression like *I ate, I eat, I will eat,* (Simple Past, Simple Present, Simple Future), or, alternatively, *I was eating, I am eating* and *I will be eating* (Progressive Past, Progressive Present, Progressive Future). Avoid mixing types of tenses in chronological sequences.

> Examples.

Bad: The work crew is scheduled to begin clearing the site on Monday. The work includes cutting down trees, removal of large rocks and to level the site.

Good: **The work crew is scheduled to begin clearing the site on Monday. The work includes cutting down trees, removing large rocks and leveling the site.**

Bad: Our company policy does not permit employees who work overtime to take regular work hours off as compensation, or getting paid more than their regular hourly rates.

Good: **Our company policy does not permit employees who work overtime to take regular work hours off as compensation, or to get paid more than their regular hourly rates.**

Bad: During their first year with the company new employees are expected to come early, be working hard and stays late.

Good: **During their first year with the company new employees are expected to come early, work hard and stay late.**

Bad: They are digging foundations at the building site when they found what appeared to be remains of a human skeleton. Everyone is relieved to find out the bones turned out to be the remains of a deer.

Good: **They were digging foundations at the building site when they found what appeared to be remains of a human skeleton. Everyone was relieved to find out the bones were the remains of a deer.**

I. PRINCIPLE OF COHESIVENESS – C. PARAGRAPH LEVEL.
c. BE CONSISTENT

(30)   Avoid Shifts in Subject.

Our rule here, also involved with *avoiding structural shifts,* concerns the need to make sure we stick with the original subject when we make references to it later in the sentence, or in other sentences in the paragraph. This is often an error of assumptions, where we, as writers of the text, assume one idea, though the readers may assume something completely different. Shifts in subject reference often come from the combining of two sentences that don't fit well together, and often seem to leave some sort of transitionary element out. For example, if we are discussing the quality of a company's product in one clause, it is confusing to then refer to the company's reputation in the next, as the following example illustrates.

Bad: ABM's portable *computers* are very easy to use, because *it* is an excellent company.
Good: ABM's portable *computers* are very easy to use, because *they* are very well made.

The general rule of thumb, when you have complex subjects, is that the last noun of the subject phrase is the main subject (**computers**, in the examples, above). This is not always the case, but in general, adjectives usually are placed **before** the nouns that they modify.
Some complex subjects contain verbs which are used to modify the subjects. For these sentences too, however, the rule is the same, the explanatory clauses should refer to the main subject, and not a part of the subject phrase (for example, the verb) which simply modifies the subject.

Bad: ABM's new processing *computers* is a lot of fun.
Good: ABM's new processing *computers* are a lot of fun to use.

However, when the subject is the action (the verb) and not the thing that is being acted upon, then the explanatory phrase must refer to the verb in subject position.

Good: *Using* ABM's new portable computers *is* a lot of fun.

> Examples.

Bad: All employees are expected to use the guidelines listed in the new employee's handbook to conduct themselves appropriately during business hours. It should be read by all full time and part time staff.

Good: **All employees are expected to use the guidelines in the new employee's handbook to conduct themselves appropriately during business hours. The guidelines should be read by all full time and part time staff.**
(or)

Good: **All employees are expected to use the new employee's handbook to conduct themselves appropriately during business hours. It should be read by all full time and part time staff.**

Bad: I have just read the fax sent to us from Star Systems in New Jersey, which is a place I have not yet visited.

Good: **I have just read the fax sent to us from Star Systems in New Jersey. I was reminded of the fact that I still have not visited our offices in New Jersey.**

Bad: The Yabe Rice Crackers Store sell not only rice crackers, but roasted chestnuts as well. We are conveniently located near the Tawaramachi Station of the Ginza subway line. Stop by and see us the next time you are visiting the Asakusa Shrine.

Good: **The Yabe Rice Crackers Store sells not only rice crackers, but roasted chestnuts as well. We are conveniently located near the Tawaramachi Station of the Ginza subway line. Stop by and see us the next time you are visiting the Asakusa Shrine.**

I. PRINCIPLE OF COHESIVENESS – C. PARAGRAPH LEVEL.
c. BE CONSISTENT

(31)   Keep References, Labels, Units of Measurement Consistent.

Once you have determined exactly who your audience is, and the level of formality and technicality that you believe best fits your audience, then it is best to stay within the parameters you have established for yourself (remember, avoid mixing common terms with technical terms).

Units of measurement are perhaps the most difficult to get straight. While most of the world has adopted the metric system, the U.S. has yet to do so in most areas. What this means is that terms that are familiar to you may not be familiar to your audience, so be prepared to offer simple conversions for your most important units of measurement. Beyond that, though, it is important to not mix the types of measurements, and to also avoid mixing the levels of whatever standards you do decide to adopt. For example, don't mix inches with centimeters, miles with kilometers, ounces with milliliters, and so forth. And, if you have chosen to use a particular standard of measurement, such as meters, to describe lengths of wood, for example, decide on a standard level of cut off (decide on whether you are going to use tenths, hundredths, etc.,) and keep these standards the same throughout your text.

References are the terms you use to refer to technical items in your text. For example, in a discussion on medical supplies, you need to decide whether you are going to use the technical terms (for example, the ingredients in a drug, such as *acetaminophen*) for the medicines you describe, or the laymen terms (such as the product name, *Tylenol*®). Again, once you have made the decision, consistently adhere to these forms throughout the text.

Labels are quite similar to references, and are simply the terms you use to designate frequently referred to items. Using the medical terminology once again, you need to decide whether you will employ the common terms such as *pills*, or slightly less common terms such as *tablets*, or even quite uncommon terms such as *oral medication pellets* (this last example is most definitely *not* Plain Written English).

> Examples.

Bad: Since the cost of acetaminophen has risen nearly thirty percent over the last year, I would like the research department to see whether we can reduce the size of our tablets from the current 500 mg per tablet to something like .325 g.

Good: **Since the cost of acetaminophen has risen nearly thirty percent over the last year, I would like the research department to see whether we can reduce the size of our tablets from the current 500 mg per tablet to something like 325 mg.**

Bad: Our current line of cosmetics include nail polishes, lip sticks, facial creams, and other make up items. I would like us to consider adding stuff for hair as well.

Good: **Our current line of cosmetics include nail polishes, lip sticks, facial creams, and other make up items. I would like us to consider adding shampoo and other hair grooming items as well.**

Bad: The new Toyonda Mark 5 Sedan gets excellent gas mileage, and has an extended trip capacity. The Mark 5 was tested at 42 mph/gallon on the highway, 29 mph/gallon in the city. Further, due to an enlarged gas tank, the Mark 5 can now travel nearly 500 km between fill ups, when driven on the open road.

Good: **The new Toyonda Mark 5 Sedan gets excellent gas mileage, and has an extended trip capacity. The Mark 5 was tested at 42 mph/gallon on the highway, 29 mph/gallon in the city. Further, due to an enlarged gas tank, the Mark 5 can now travel more than 300 miles between fill ups, when driven on the open road.**

Bad: To make the inexpensive adhesive, just mix flour and H^2O together, in equal parts.

Good: **To make the inexpensive glue, just mix flour and water together, in equal parts.**

I. PRINCIPLE OF COHESIVENESS – C. PARAGRAPH LEVEL.
d. AVOID DISTRACTIONS

(32) Avoid Needless Repetition of Words.

This is an important rule, and needs to be employed in virtually everything you write. Another way of phrasing this is simply *Use Diversity in Word Selection*. This rule does not mean that we must find unusual, uncommon or fancy words to add to our text. Rather, it simply means that we should avoid repetition of the same words over and over again throughout our text. Of course there are times when repetition of a particular point is necessary, as when we want to emphasize something, or remind our reader of an earlier point. For the most part, however, we want to vary our word choice to keep the audience from getting bored. Two main areas can be addressed here, one, in the word selection of *content* words (nouns, adjectives, adverbs and verbs) and the other in the choice of *function* words (prepositions, articles, etc.).

The repetition of the same *content* words throughout a text gives off the impression that the writer lacks imagination, creativity or worse, intelligence. Repeated words also serve to make the text seem longer and more monotonous that necessary, and should be avoided. Usually there are several other suitable common words for any one that is repeated. Frequently repeated content words (or their substitutes) include *said, it, thing, they*, etc.

Bad: *Late summer* is a busy time for rice farmers in Japan since it is in *late summer* that the rice must be harvested.

Good: *Late summer* is a busy time for rice farmers in Japan since *it* is then that the rice must be harvested.

Similarly, repetition of *function* words can and should be avoided. Function words that are frequently repeated more than they should include: *said, it, and, things, so, also, by* and so forth. A significant number of suitable alternatives can be found for virtually any other frequently used function word. Again, this kind of repetition is particularly distracting in a sentence (since words are so close to each other, and thus, the repetition is readily apparent), but is also a problem at the paragraph level. We often don't notice the repetition when we write, so be sure to look for repeated words when you proofread your text.

> Examples.

Bad: The boss said that we were all doing a good job. He also said that he hoped that we wouldn't have to continue working nights anymore, and he said that from now on, overtime would be paid at double your normal rates. He also said that we would be hiring some additional staff over the next few months.

Good: **The boss said that we were all doing a good job. He also mentioned that he hoped that we wouldn't have to continue working nights anymore, and that from now on, overtime would be paid at double your normal rates. He added that we would be hiring some additional staff over the next few months.**

Bad: Things have been quite busy lately, and lots of things have been left undone until now. I hope to deal with some of the more important things here in this memo, and later, I will address some of the smaller things with each of your personally.

Good: **I have been quite busy lately, and lots of things have been left undone until now. I hope to deal with some of the more important issues here in this memo, and later, I will address some of the smaller items with each of your personally.**

Bad: First, I would all of you write down any suggestions you might have. Then, I would like you to discuss these suggestions at each of your team meetings. Then, I want you to meet together, just the supervisors, and see if you can agree on one or two of the ideas. Then, I want you to report back to me with your best proposal.

Good: **First, I would all of you write down any suggestions you might have. Next, I would like you to discuss these suggestions at each of your team meetings. After that, I want you to meet together, just the supervisors, and see if you can agree on one or two of the ideas. Finally, I want you to report back to me with your best proposal.**

II. PRINCIPLE OF DIRECTNESS.

Overview

The next 16 rules in this text are all rules which support the **Principle of Directness.** This principle is also used for spoken English as well, and essentially, the rules here help us to direct the audience to the pertinent information, with as little deviation as possible. There are four basic rules supporting the Principle of Directness: 1) *State what things are, not what they seem to be;* 2) *State the subject clearly;* 3) *State the "bottom line" succinctly;* 4) *Avoid negatives.* Not all of the rules are used at each of the three levels of text (word, sentence and paragraph), as explained below.

The first rule of the Principle of Directness, ***State what things are, not what they seem to be,*** is a rule that is employed at all levels of text development. This rule emphasizes the need to state facts, as opposed to assumptions. It encourages concreteness in terms as well as ideas. Further, a key element of this rule is to avoid ambiguity, ambiguity which can arise out of poor word choice, loose grammatical structure, and unknown or uncommon references.

The second rule, ***State the subject clearly,*** is also used in all three levels of text development. At the word level, we want to be clear about exactly what the subject is, and refer to it by using concrete content words, rather than indeterminate pronouns such as *it* or *this*. At the sentence level, this rule is used to encourage linking pronouns clearly to the words they refer to. Also, we look at the confusion that arises when key words are left out of our basic sentence, and finally, we look at how the sense of a sentence can be changed quite dramatically by the placement of modifiers such as adverbs and adjectives. This is an important issue, and involves the understanding and use of *scope*.

The third rule, ***State the "bottom line" succinctly***, is logically employed only at the paragraph level. This is a rule which governs the placement and ordering of information and has been dealt with extensively in the discussion involving the Principle of Cohesiveness. Here we add to this discussion a point about not going into great detail on issues or points that you intend to later dismiss.

Finally, the fourth rule, ***Avoid negatives***, is used at both the sentence and paragraph levels of development (and really, at the word choice level as well). Basically, here we are encouraged to avoid using directly negative terms and expressions that are not neutral. We need to be careful of our tone and attitude as well, so that the readers are not misled or distracted from the points that we are intending to communicate.

II. PRINCIPLE OF DIRECTNESS – A. WORD LEVEL.
a. STATE WHAT THINGS ARE, NOT WHAT THEY SEEM TO BE

(33)   Use Concrete Terms.

In order to be direct and to the point, it is important to begin by choosing words that are clear and concrete, preferably with a single definite reference. This is very important in business writing, and deviates significantly from various literary styles of expression.

Words and phrases that should generally be avoided in this context include *think, believe, seems, seems as if, appears, appears to be, looks like, looks as if* and any other terms that convey the idea of uncertainty or ambiguity. This is particularly relevant to discussions of a factual nature, such as an analysis of a new experimental procedure, a summary of issues that need to be resolved, a review of current inventory, a discussion concerning supplies, resources, and so forth. If, for example, you are proposing a new model to replace an older design, you would want to avoid references like *the new model seems to outperform the older one,* or, *the new model looks like it could last longer that the original model.* These statements should be said more directly and more concretely. The new model either out performs the older one, or it doesn't, and similarly, the new model either lasts longer, or it doesn't. Both statements could be made more concrete by simply stating what things are, not what they seem to be *(the new model clearly out performs the older one, or, the new model definitely last longer that the original model.).*

There are of course situations where you need to convey a degree of uncertainty. We often discuss the weather in such a manner (*It looks like it is going to rain,* or, *It seems like this is going to be another cold summer*). These examples are statements of pure speculation, and have no facts to support them, so naturally they should be stated with some degree of uncertainty. However, even these statements are fairly direct, as opposed to a statement like *Does anybody think the offices are not heated well enough?*, where the actual intended message is, *I would like to suggest that we raise the temperatures in the offices.* The second statement removes any doubt as to what our intended message is, while the first statement leaves it up to the audience to try and figure out for themselves.

> Examples.

Bad: The Star Systems new co-processor appears to be the fastest co-processor on the market today.

Good: The Star Systems new co-processor is the fastest co-processor on the market today.

Bad: I think your proposal is worth considering, please write it up in detail.

Good: Your proposal is worth considering, please write it up in detail.

Bad: The new blend rice doesn't seem like it is very popular with sushi shop owners.

Good: The new blend rice isn't very popular with sushi shop owners.

Bad: I believe that we should spend the extra money so that we can get an extended service contract.

Good: We should spend the extra money so that we can get an extended service contract.

Bad: Is anybody really interested in doing business with the bankrupt Mechanical Foresight firm?

Good: We are not interested in doing business with the bankrupt Mechanical Foresight firm.

Bad: It looks like there might be a problem with the placement of the gas tank in the new design.

Good: There is a problem with the placement of the gas tank in the new design.

II. PRINCIPLE OF DIRECTNESS – A. WORD LEVEL.
a. STATE WHAT THINGS ARE, NOT WHAT THEY SEEM TO BE

(34)   Avoid Lexical Ambiguity.

Ambiguity is confusion or uncertainty regarding the intended meaning of a message. Ambiguity can be caused by many different factors, including poor sentence structure, poor word choice, unclear reference to prior information, and so forth. Here, we will focus on semantic ambiguity (words with indefinite meanings) and categorical ambiguity (words that are both nouns and verbs).

Many words are ambiguous simply because they are too general, or, have several distinct meanings. Words such as this include *people, man, dish, good, hot, hard,* and other very common words. For example, when would you use the word *people*? Perhaps if you are talking about developing a new item on the menu of a restaurant, you might write something like, *I think people will be very interested in this dish.* Are we thinking of potential customers? If so, why not simply use the more direct, concrete term, *customer*? Similarly, for the sentence above, the word dish is a poor word choice, since even in the context of restaurants and food preparation, there are two clear possible things which it can refer to (a *type of meal*, and a *plate*).

Other examples of words that have more than one meaning, such as *dish*, above, include both nouns and verbs. For example, the sentence *Mary licked her wounds* could refer to the situation where *Mary's wounds healed successfully*, or, alternatively, *Mary used her tongue to actually lick the exposed sores* (yuk!). Similarly, in the sentence *Mary can't bear children,* we are faced with two choices, *Mary is not able to conceive a child,* or, *Mary doesn't like children.* A final example should suffice to ensure our understanding of our rule here: *Smoking grass can be nauseating.* Here, we either mean that *the act of one actually smoking cigarettes made out of grass (by inhaling smoke) can make you sick,* or simply, *a pile of grass that is smoldering can make you sick.* Again, to avoid lexical ambiguity, use specific concrete terms, instead of words with general or multiple meanings.

> Examples.

Bad: The new supervisor's appointment was shocking to the staff.

Good: **The appointment that the new supervisor made was shocking to the staff.**
(or)
Good: **The staff was shocked when they learned who was appointed to be their new supervisor.**

Bad: I think you will all agree that our new chicken sandwich is very hot.

Good: **I think you will all agree that our new chicken sandwich is very popular.**

Bad: The horses will be well fed and prepared to ride.

Good: **The horses will be well fed and prepared for transport by train.**

Bad: I was told by the president that he finally decided on the boat.

Good: **I was told by the president that he finally decided on purchasing the boat.**
(or)
Good: **I was told by the president that he finally decided on making the purchase while he was on the boat.**

Bad: The hot dogs are ready to eat.

Good: **The hot dogs are cooked and ready to eat.**
(or)
Good: **(After chasing cattle all morning) the hot and tired dogs are ready to eat.**

II. PRINCIPLE OF DIRECTNESS – A. WORD LEVEL.
b. STATE THE SUBJECT CLEARLY

(35)   Avoid Indirect and Unspecific Subject and Object Reference.

At the word level, we want to choose terms for the subject (and the object) that are clear and concrete. We focus specifically on the subject and object here because these are critical elements of any sentence, and any paragraph, and are areas where we can use subject *substitutes* such as personal pronouns (*I, we, he, she, they, us, them, her,* etc.), demonstrative pronouns (*this, that, those,* etc.), indefinite pronouns (*one, none, any, everyone, anybody, everybody,* etc.), and the existential function words (*here* and *there*). As a general rule of word choice, *we never begin a topic sentence with any of these noun substitutes other than those that refer to the first person (I, we, us, our).* This rule is particularly important for the first sentence of the first paragraph of any text, but it is a useful rule to follow elsewhere in the text as well. As an illustration of this point, in the old (1979) movie Star Trek® The Motion Picture, Captain Kirk says to one of his officers, "There's a thing out there, headed this way." This line is delivered for its humorous impact, since it is said in the context of a highly sophisticated, technologically advanced space ship, and it is a perfect example of unspecific and unclear reference. The humor is in the fact that the informal statement is completely opposite to what we would expect.

As we saw in the last rule, some nouns are unspecific and indirect as well. For example, in addition to the words listed in the last rule, nouns such as *reports, sources, expenses, work, job, task, office, company* are all too general for many purposes, and should be replaced by more specific references, or modified by adjectives to more clearly indicate what is being referred to. For example, if I began a memo with the sentence **The report indicated that there will be an increased workload*, the reader will surely have some questions: *Which report?*; *Does more work mean more pay?*; *Is this a good thing or a bad thing?*, and so forth. These questions could have been prevented by better word selection:

Good: *The Kinnel Report indicated that we will need to hire more staff.*

> Examples.

Bad: The one who came before the second one is the one you need to consult with.

Good: You need to consult with the original personnel representative, not her replacement.

Bad: I would like to order the things we discussed at our last meeting.

Good: I would like to order the stereo headphones and mini amplifiers that we discussed at our last meeting.

Bad: That building will have to be repainted before we can think about renting it out again.

Good: The building on 4th and Main will have to be repainted before we can think about renting it out again.

Bad: Sources indicate that we will need to order replacement parts for the printing presses much sooner than we thought.

Good: The print shop supervisor said that we will need to order replacement parts for the printing presses much sooner than we thought.

Bad: After the tasks are completed, everyone is expected to help with clean up.

Good: After you have finished the tasks specifically assigned to you, you are expected to help with clean up.

II. PRINCIPLE OF DIRECTNESS – B. WORD LEVEL.
a. STATE WHAT THINGS ARE, NOT WHAT THEY SEEM TO BE

(36) <u>State What Things Are, Not What They Seem to Be.</u>

This rule at the sentence level is meant to discourage writers from making statements that are merely assumptions, or common beliefs, and treat them as facts. It is easy for those of us who are authorities in our given fields to develop beliefs, attitudes, intuitions, perceptions, expectations and such that are the result of our close contact with our chosen profession. So, one consequence of this rule is to require clarification as to whether your statements are the generally accepted truth, your own personally held convictions, or facts supported by documented evidence. We will pursue this last point more thoroughly at the paragraph level. What we will address here in more detail is separating true facts from common beliefs.

Common beliefs are the things that everyone within a particular group generally holds to be true, and are not specifically your personal opinions. These kinds of beliefs are often attributed to indefinite sources as "they say," "I have heard," "as you know," and the like. When you find yourself writing statements that have indefinite sources such as this, it is best to rethink the statements and see if you can either change them into one of personal opinion (see rule #20 for related discussion), or attribute the statements to a legitimate and recognizable source. If neither of these alternatives seem appropriate, then it is usually best to simply leave out such statements, and focus on the facts that you do know, and opinions that you are comfortable with.

If you do choose to state your opinions, make sure that you have exercised the appropriate options to determine if the opinions are valid or not. In other words, if you are writing about the postal regulations for importing used photo equipment, and you are aware of the charges for importing new equipment, but not for used, you may be inclined to assume that there will be no differences between the two, and state in your text that they are the same. However, this is the kind of thing that can be verified fairly easily, and as such, should not be simply your assumption. So, whenever possible, state the facts, not what you *think* the facts might be.

Examples.

Bad: They say that it is very difficult to get into the Japanese market, but I don't agree.

Good: **The U.S. Foreign Business Administration says that it is very difficult to get into the Japanese market, but I don't agree.**

Bad: As you know, prices in Tokyo are sometimes quite cheap compared to the cost of similar items in other cities in Southern and Northern Japan.

Good: **According to the Yomiuri Shimbun, prices in Tokyo are sometimes quite cheap compared to the cost of identical items in other cities in Southern and Northern Japan.**

Bad: I have heard that it is easy to import goods from other countries if they are used, but not if they are new.

Good: **It is easy to import goods from other countries if they are used, but not if they are new.**

Bad: I learned that they charge an import tax on mail order shoes that is nearly equal to the cost of the shoes.

Good: **The Japanese government regulates the purchasing of mail order shoes by imposing substantial importation fees.**

Bad: Everyone knows that the reason the business failed is because of its poor location.

Good: **Clearly, the business failed because of its poor location.**

II. PRINCIPLE OF DIRECTNESS – B. SENTENCE LEVEL.
a. STATE WHAT THINGS ARE, NOT WHAT THEY SEEM TO BE

(37)   Avoid Syntactic Ambiguity.

Syntactic ambiguity refers to confusion that arises as a result of poor sentence structure. Confusion usually arises from a sentence that has more than one interpretation. Syntactic ambiguity can be caused by poor word choice, by poor placement (or sequencing) of phrases, by incorrect placement of modifiers (adverbs and adjectives) and by the omission of key words in a sentence. All of these issues are dealt with separately in this text, but for our purposes here, we will focus on sentences that are grammatically correct, but may have several interpretations because of poor word choice, and poor phrasal juxtaposition.

To illustrate, look over the following sentences, all of which contain one form of ambiguity or another.

Bad: The professor found a book on Martin Luther King Boulevard.
Bad: Michiko lectured on Martin Luther King Boulevard.
Bad: They are moving sidewalks.
Bad: Terry loves his wife and so do I.

For the first example, *the professor was either walking on King Boulevard and found a book on the ground*, or, *he was in a library and found a book that was written about King boulevard*. In the first interpretation, the phrase beginning with *on* modifies the subject, the *professor*, by describing his location, while in the second interpretation, the *on*-phrase modifies the object, the book, by describing the type of book. Similarly, in the second example, *Michiko* was either *on the boulevard at the time that she lectured*, or presumably elsewhere, where *she gave a lecture with the boulevard as its theme*. For the third example, some *group of workers are taking the sidewalks from one location and placing them in another*, or, *the sidewalks themselves move* (like "people transports" at airports). For the last example, we have either *Terry loves his wife and I love my wife*, or, *Terry loves his wife, and I love Terry's wife too*. In general, syntactic ambiguity can be avoided by a combination of proper word choice, straightforward organization of phrases and a few well placed modifiers.

> Examples.

Bad: It is easy to play ragtime on this piano. [no focus]

Good: **Ragtime is easy to play on this piano.** [focus on *ragtime*, a type of music]
(or)
Good: **This piano is easy to play Ragtime on.** [focus on *piano*, this one is easier than others)]

Bad: The Yakuza has requested protection from attacks by the police.

Good: **The Yakuza asked the police for protection from attacks.**
(or)
Good: **The Yakuza asked someone for protection from police attacks.**

Bad: A minister married my sister.

Good: **My sister is married to a minister.**
(or)
Good: **A minister performed the wedding ceremony at my sister's wedding.**

Bad: John loves Susan more than Marsha.

Good: **John loves Susan and Marsha loves Susan, but Marsha doesn't love Susan as much as John loves Susan.**
(or)
Good: **John loves Susan and Marsha, but John loves Susan more than he loves Marsha.**

Bad: Batman hit the villain with gloves.

Good: **Batman hit the villain who was wearing gloves.**
(or)
Good: **Batman used his gloves to hit the villain.**

II. PRINCIPLE OF DIRECTNESS – B. SENTENCE LEVEL.
b. STATE THE SUBJECT CLEARLY

(38)   Replace Adverbial and Adjectival Phrases with Single Adverbs or Adjectives.

Adverbial and adjectival phrases are phrases made up of abstract nouns and adverbs and/or adjectives. These include expressions such as "in close proximity," "in the near future," or "an offensive nature," and "to a certain degree," and so forth. In the interest of both Directness and Economy, we can replace these wordy phrases with single adjectives and adverbs without detracting from the inherent meanings of the longer expressions.

Bad	Good
in close juxtaposition	**close, or, near**
in a confident manner	**confidently**
on a permanent basis	**permanently**
in an offensive nature	**offensively**
a high degree of dexterity	**dexterously**
a very remote possibility	**unlikely**

Adverbial phrases often come in the form of dependent clauses, using the progressive form of a verb (for example, "after eating breakfast," or "before going to work". In these cases, it is difficult to reduce the clauses to single adverbs. Rather, the concern we have here is simply placing them correctly in a sentence. The easiest rule for the placement adverbial phrases in sentences is to simply put them first, before the main independent clause, and as a second option, place it last, after the independent clause. In other words, it is best to avoid placing the adverbial phrase of this type inside of the independent clause. By doing so will unnecessarily confuse the syntax. Some adverbial phrases, such as "on Friday," or "after the game" do not contain the progressive verb forms as discussed above, but also follow the same basic rules of placement (before or after the main independent clause).

> Examples.

Bad: I ate the cheese which I bought yesterday this afternoon.

Good: This afternoon I ate the cheese which I bought yesterday.

Bad: I drove back as soon as I heard the news in a cautious manner.

Good: As soon as I heard the news I drove back cautiously.

Bad: We look forward to working with you in the future and at once will send out your order.

Good: We look forward to working with you in the future and will send out your order at once.

Bad: They have increased their sales over the last two or three years or so at a slow degree of speed.

Good: Over the last two or three years or so their sales have slowly increased.

Bad: Yesterday, though I rarely eat out anymore, I had dinner at Alioto's.

Good: Though I rarely eat out anymore, yesterday I had dinner at Alioto's.
(or)
Good: Though I rarely eat out anymore, I had dinner at Alioto's yesterday.

Bad: I heard just now today they are arriving at noon.

Good: Just now I heard that they are arriving today at noon.

II. PRINCIPLE OF DIRECTNESS – B. SENTENCE LEVEL.
b. STATE THE SUBJECT CLEARLY

(39)   Using Scope to Avoid Misplaced Adverbs.

Scope refers to the range that an adverb can have an effect on within a sentence. Generally, adverbs that occur early in a sentence have the potential of having a greater range of effect than ones occurring late in the sentence. Negatives, too, can have a similar impact. The solution to confusion resulting from misplaced modifiers is to place the modifier as close as possible to the word that it is modifying, or, alternatively, to change the order of phrases so it is clear that one modifier cannot modify another.

Let's begin by looking at scope in the placement of the adverb *nearly*. We can place this adverb at two locations within a sentence, but each placement results in a different interpretation of the sentence meaning.

The boss *nearly* spent a thousand dollars on a new fax machine.

The boss spent *nearly* a thousand dollars on a new fax machine.

For these last two examples, "nearly spent" could refer to a situation where *he almost bought the fax machine, but he did not*, or, alternatively, *the boss spent a lot of money on the fax machine, in fact, he spent almost one thousand dollars*. So, for the first example, placement of the adverb *nearly* before the verb ("spent"), and further from the dollar figure, leaves the sentence open to confusion as an ambiguous structure. In the second sentence, however, *nearly* follows the verb, and it is clear the boss actually spent the money, almost one thousand dollars. This is an example where adverb placement has narrowed the scope, which in turn reduces ambiguity. Often the easiest way to avoid this kind of confusion is to leave out the modifiers entirely. Other adverbs which are used in this way include *only, merely, simply, also, even* and *mainly*.

Sometimes, whole phrases seem out of place, and create unnecessary confusion. When this occurs, it is usually quite easy just to move phrases around to make things clear.

Bad: When just thirty years old, my dad helped me to start my own company. Who was thirty years old, 'me' or 'my Dad'? It is unclear, so it is best to rearrange things.

Good: When I was just thirty years old, my Dad helped me to start my own company.

> Examples.

Bad: Almost the entire company went bankrupt. *(means that most of the company went bankrupt)*

Good: The entire company almost went bankrupt. *(means that the company did not go bankrupt)*

Bad: Senior staff members are only invited to the dinner. (they aren't invited to anything else)

Good: Only senior staff members are invited to the dinner. (no one else is invited)

Bad: Even the company offered to pay to clean up the river.

Good: The company even offered to pay to clean up the river.

Bad: They spent nearly a whole month longer than expected to complete the highway repairs.

Bad: They nearly spent a whole month longer than expected to complete the highway repairs.

Good: They spent a whole month longer than expected to complete the highway repairs.
(or)
Good: They spent about one month longer than expected to complete the highway repairs.

Bad: He reported simply that they would look into the problem.

Bad: He simply reported that they would look into the problem.

Good: He reported that they would look into the problem.

II. PRINCIPLE OF DIRECTNESS – B. SENTENCE LEVEL.
b. STATE THE SUBJECT CLEARLY

(40)   Avoid Subject Ambiguity by Using the Correct Personal Pronouns.

It is a common mistake to use the wrong pronoun in English for the simple fact that there are so many of them. There are *subjective* pronouns, *objective* pronouns, and *reflexive* pronouns to name the most common ones.

The *subjective* pronouns are used as noun substitutes to refer to nouns that have already been mentioned in the text. The pronouns include the singular *I, you, he, she, it* and the plural *we, you* and *they*. When asking about the identity of the subject, the subjective question word is *who*: *I wrote Francis a long letter. We will visit Paula this afternoon. Who told the employees to work overtime?*

The *objective* pronouns, on the other hand, are used to refer to nouns in the object position (singular: *me, you, him, her* and *it*; plural: *us, you* and *them*). The question word for asking about the identity of person as the object is *whom*: *Seiichi wrote him a long letter. The managers will visit her this afternoon. The boss told whom to work overtime?* Notice that the question words, *who* and *whom*, can be used to refer to both singular and plural nouns (in Modern English you will find that *who* is often used instead of *whom*, and that you can usually make good sentences without ever using the less common *whom*).

When there are several individuals that comprise either the subject or the object, the rules remain unchanged. If you are referring to a member in the subject group, then use the appropriate subjective pronoun. Likewise, if you are referring to a member in the group that make up the object, then use an objective pronoun: *Seiichi and I visited Paula this afternoon.* (Subjective *I*) and; *Seiichi visited Paula and me earlier this afternoon.* (Objective *me*)

An easy way to test whether you have chosen the correct pronoun or not is to split the sentence into two equal statements, if both are correct independently, then you have chosen the right pronoun. The sentence *Seiichi and I visited Paula this afternoon,* can be split into: *(1) Seiichi visited Paula this afternoon. (2) I visited Paula this afternoon.* (not *Me visited Paula this afternoon.)

> Examples.

Bad: The board members and me have decided to extend the maternity leave policy to a full six months off with guaranteed reemployment rights.

Good: **The board members and I have decided to extend the maternity leave policy to a full six months off with guaranteed reemployment rights.**

Bad: If you have any questions concerning the new pay schedule, Ms. Suzuki is now in charge of handling this area. I suggest he write to you directly.

Good: **If you have any questions concerning the new pay schedule, Ms. Suzuki is now in charge of handling this area. I suggest you write to her directly.**

Bad: The inspectors will want to talk to she about the missing money.

Good: **The inspectors will want to talk to her about the missing money.**

Bad: The management voted to give Mr. Kant and I a raise.

Good: **The management voted to give Mr. Kant and me a raise.**

Bad: To who did they give the new title of "first secretary to the vice president"?

Good: **To whom did they give the new title of "first secretary to the vice president"?**

Bad: Please return the complete questionnaire to I or Mr. Matsumoto.

Good: **Please return the complete questionnaire to me or Mr. Matsumoto.**

II. PRINCIPLE OF DIRECTNESS – B. SENTENCE LEVEL.
b. STATE THE SUBJECT CLEARLY

(41)   Avoid Subject and Object Ambiguity by Using Reflexive Pronouns Correctly.

Reflexive pronouns include the singular *myself, yourself, himself, herself* and *itself*, and the plural *ourselves, yourselves* and *themselves*. The main use of reflexive pronouns is to show *agreement* between the subject and the object, while a secondary use of the pronouns is to place *emphasis* on the subject. These pronouns should not be confused with the genitive, or possessive pronouns (*mine, ours, hers,* etc.), since these do not refer to agents involved in some form of action, as the reflexives do.

Using reflexive pronouns to indicate *agreement* between the subject and the object is done by placing a pronoun in object position that refers to the same entity as the subject. This pronoun, then, agrees in number and person with the subject, reflecting its origin back to the subject noun. In a real sense, then, this use of the reflexive also emphasizes the subject, by identifying the object with it. In other words, the subject does an action where the object of the action is the same as the subject.

I gave myself a raise.

Most employees would rather not have to pay for the own health benefits themselves.

The boss expects everyone, including himself, to work overtime.

In each of the examples, above, the reflexive pronouns refer to the main subjects, though they are in a position following the main verb, and as such, are in basic object positions. Therefore, the objects and subjects are in agreement.

On the other hand, when we want to *emphasize* that the subject, too, is involved in the main action, then we place the reflexive pronoun in a position that follows the main subject (a position of *focus*), but precedes the main verb.

The boss himself was the one to tell us the bad news.

I, myself, voted against the new benefits package.

This use of reflexives to indicate emphasis is similar to using a word such as *even*, as in *even the boss* (instead of *the boss himself*), or, *too*, as in *I, too,* (instead of *I, myself,*).

> Examples.

Bad: The invitation is open to all employees and their spouses, everyone is expected to enjoy yourselves at the company's expense.

Good: The invitation is open to all employees and their spouses, everyone is expected to enjoy themselves at the company's expense.

Bad: The convention itselves is designed to be an example of excellent organization.

Good: The convention itself is designed to be an example of excellent organization.

Bad: Each employee is expected to look after his desk, his office and his locker theirselves.

Good: Each employee is expected to look after his desk, his office and his locker himself.

Bad: I even me have tried the toothpaste, and I think that it is excellent.

Good: I myself have tried the toothpaste, and I think that it is excellent.

Bad: Even herself the secretary stated that she did not like the new computers.

Good: Even the secretary herself stated that she did not like the new computers.

Bad: Everyone is responsible for cleaning out their own lockers theirselves.

Good: Everyone is responsible for cleaning out their own lockers themselves.

II. PRINCIPLE OF DIRECTNESS – B. SENTENCE LEVEL.
c. AVOID NEGATIVES WHENEVER POSSIBLE

(42)   Avoid Negative Expressions and Double Negatives.

Rarely does a business text benefit from <u>extensive</u> use of *no, don't, can't, not* and so forth (even words like *never* and *wrong* are usually too direct, and thus unsuitable). In virtually any situation, there is a way to say the things that you want to say, without using words that have negative connotations, and therefore will not have unpleasant ramifications. Negatives are necessary at times, however. For example, if you are describing a system of rules and regulations, or other messages such as warnings about various hazards, then negatives are to be expected. Even here, though, instead of saying "*don't* do such and such," we can usually rephrase our comments in a positive way, by saying, for example, "*it is best to do* such and such." It is best to avoid negatives especially in the area of discussing the quality of someone's work, telling people whether their requests can be honored, etc. (i.e., comments that are *directed to individuals*).

Sometimes, too, using terms such as *not* renders your text <u>vague and lacking of clear purpose or commitment.</u> For example:
Bad: He has not done the kind of work that we wanted him to do.
Good: His work has been poor and needs to be improved.
So, the use of *not* can create an unpleasant mood in your text, it can confuse the reader because of problems with scope, and it can also indicate a certain degree of indecisiveness. When you have a choice between using *not* and a verb (or adjective), or using another verb that says the same thing, use the alternative without *no* or *not*. Here are just a few examples.

<u>Bad</u>	<u>**Good**</u>
not decisive	**indecisive**
not willing	**unwilling**
didn't leave	**stayed**
don't use	**avoid**
didn't respond	**remained silent**
don't accept	**refuse**

Double negatives, on the other hand, are simply too difficult to understand for the most part, and should always be avoided (i.e., it is like the rule of physics: "two negatives make a positive"). For example, *I was not unwilling to go*, could be stated much more clearly as *I was willing to go*. Other examples include *reliable* (for *not unreliable*), *patient* (for *not impatient*), *possible* (for *not impossible*), and so forth.

Examples.

Bad: Do not continue to try to sell us sloppily constructed goods.

Good: We are interested in goods meeting the highest quality standards.

Bad: You are not right when you say that we do not pay our bills on time.

Good: You are incorrect when you say that we do not pay our bills on time.

Bad: We are not unopposed to a merger, but we need more time to study our options.

Good: A merger might be a possibility, but we need more time to study our options.

Bad: You did not do it the way that I wanted.

Good: I think there is a better way to do it. Let me show you.

Bad: As our newest member, you're wrong more often than you are right, why don't you just listen for a change?

Good: Since you're still new here, I think it would be best if you just listened and followed along for a while.

Bad: Your memos are not decisive enough. You must not avoid stating things exactly as you see them.

Good: Your memos are indecisive. You should state things exactly as you see them.

II. PRINCIPLE OF DIRECTNESS – C. PARAGRAPH LEVEL.
a. STATE WHAT THINGS ARE, NOT WHAT THEY SEEM TO BE

(43)   Avoid Overstatement and Exaggeration.

This is a general rule of business and technical writing which serves to keep statements direct and to the point, without misstating the issues. Overstatement (and exaggeration) magnifies issues by blowing them out of proportion. It turns small problems into large ones, and it makes minor details seem as if they are important facts.

Overstatement can take many forms. One form is when a writer presents enough evidence to make a point clearly, and rather than stopping there, and moving on, the writer chooses to add even further support of his point. What began as a convincing argument turns into a tedious and unnecessarily long discussion, often rehashing over old points in slightly different ways. In essence, overstatement is the type of writing where the writer just doesn't know when to stop.

Overstatement may also result in over zealousness on the part of the writer. In this case, the writer is so excited about the topic, or so interested in convincing the readers of something, that she tries to make her case airtight, by addressing every imaginable angle. This sort of approach is rarely necessary when addressing business or technical issues, and to attempt to do so can be exhausting for the writer as well as for the reader.

Exaggeration is very similar to overstatement, and in many ways overlaps with it, however, for our purposes here, we use exaggeration to refer to *distortion*, through magnification and stretches of the imagination, of basic facts and arguments. Here, a simple example should illustrate the point. Suppose a bank manager surveyed her customers, and found that 57% desired a certain service (such as paying bills by phone). If the bank manager reported in a memo to her parent company that *the great majority of our customers expressed a desire for the option of paying bills by phone*, then her statements would be exaggerating the truth. It is best to state the facts accurately, since in business and technical applications, whatever is written down can usually be verified independently, if necessary.

Examples.

Bad: The laptop computer has become essential for performing the routine duties of our jobs here at Star Systems. I think it is time to get rid of all but a few of the desktops we have here. It is clear that no one uses their desktops at all these days, and that they just take up valuable desk space. Desktops should not be manufactured anymore, today's workplace does not require them. Star Systems should look into an efficient disposal plan, such as donation to charity, for the desktops.

Good: **The laptop computer has become essential for performing the routine duties of our jobs here at Star Systems. It is clear that no one uses their desktops at all these days, and that they just take up valuable desk space. Star Systems should look into an efficient disposal plan, such as donation to charity, for the desktops.**

- -

Bad: The engine burns fuel more efficiently than virtually anything else on the market. It is the very best engine available today.

Good: **The engine burns fuel more efficiently than virtually anything else on the market. It is the one of the best engines available today.**

- -

Bad: The new pop-top camper roof on some of the luxury vans is really just a copy of a design that a German company popularized back in the mid-seventies. The pop-top roof is not a new idea at all. In other parts of the world, it is easy to find several manufacturers producing similar types of camping and recreational vehicles. In Japan, however, the introduction of the pop-top camper roof has been treated as if it is an entirely new concept, which it is not.

Good: **The new pop-top camper roof on some of the new Japanese luxury vans is really just a copy of a design that a German company popularized back in the mid-seventies. In Japan, however, the introduction of the pop-top camper roof has been treated as if it is an entirely new concept, which it is not.**

- -

II. PRINCIPLE OF DIRECTNESS – C. PARAGRAPH LEVEL.
a. STATE WHAT THINGS ARE, NOT WHAT THEY SEEM TO BE

(44)   Separate Fact from Opinion.

When you must state your opinion (or someone else's), make sure you have followed the guidelines discussed earlier (opinions should be based upon some basic facts which can be (however indirectly) *attributable to a reputable source*, and should not be an exaggeration of these basic facts). After you have determined that your opinions meet this basic criteria, then it is very important that you *make it clear to the audience that these statements are indeed merely opinions*, and that they are clearly off-set from statements which are directly and firmly based on facts.

For the business world, since important decisions may be made based on your statements, your readers *need to know what things are and not what they seem to be*. Distinguishing between facts and opinions can be done easily by simply using a few key words and expressions such as: *I believe, in my (personal) opinion, from my perspective, as I see it (things), my idea (on the matter), in my view, from my viewpoint, a personal conviction of mine, and so forth.*

As noted previously, avoid expressions such as *appears as if, seems, looks like*, etc., unless you are discussing the probability of something happening in the future, such as making weather predictions, guesses about a company's future productivity, and so forth.

Sometimes the opinions you mention are not your own, but were originally stated by someone else. In these cases, make sure to attribute your remarks to the person who originally made the statement. The key expressions, above, need minor adjustments to make this work. For example, *in (person's name) opinion, (person's name) believes, from (company's name) perspective,* and so forth. Also, *according to* and *concurring with* are useful here. Sometimes the opinions you mention are stated on behalf of the company or organization you represent, and may or not represent your own opinions. In this situation, you can make this clear using expressions such as *speaking on behalf of, in (someone's) opinion, speaking from the perspective of (some organization),* and so forth.

> Examples.

Bad: The market for imported cheese is going to double next year.

Good: **I believe that the market for imported cheese is going to double next year.**

Bad: I am authorized to allow all employees the option of an early retirement cash out plan.

Good: **Speaking on behalf of management, I am authorized to allow all employees the option of an early retirement cash out plan.**

Bad: The owners are not likely to be interested in spending more money to get less production. However, the plan does make sense.

Good: **Speaking from the perspective of the owners, they are not likely to be interested in spending more money to get less production. However, in my personal opinion, the plan makes sense.**

Bad: Since most colleges are closed on Saturday afternoon, Hoso University is probably closed as well.

Good: **Since most colleges are closed on Saturday afternoon, I think that Hoso University is probably closed as well.**

Bad: I can tell you that you will not have to work overtime unless you want to. However, I cannot say how your not working will affect your standing in the company.

Good: **Speaking on behalf of management, I can tell you that you will not have to work overtime unless you want to. However, I do not know how your not working will affect your standing in the company.**

II. PRINCIPLE OF DIRECTNESS – C. PARAGRAPH LEVEL.
b. STATE THE SUBJECT CLEARLY

(45) Avoid Mixing Subjects and Objects up.

Sometimes it is difficult to track the subjects and objects through a paragraph, especially when various pronouns are used indiscriminately. Often it becomes confusing when one pronoun, such as "it" or "he" has several possible antecedents (original subjects to which it could refer). We have suggested earlier that one way to avoid subject reference confusion is to use pronouns correctly. There are times, though, when they shouldn't be used at all.

Note the problems of subject and object ambiguity in the following short paragraph:

Bad: Mr. Bush and Mr. Sugihara both worked on the proposal that was originally developed by Mr. Sugihara as well as one sent from the head office, but it has since undergone major changes. He wanted to add something to the basic plan, and so he helped in developing the revisions. It was a lot of work but both were pleased with the way it turned out.

In the last paragraph, it is unclear what has undergone major changes (Mr. Sugihara's plan, or the one sent from the head office), similarly, did Mr. Sugihara, or *Mr. Bush*, want to add something to the basic plan? *Which* of the two plans was the one that was revised? What does the *it* refer to, in *the way it turned out*? These kinds of problems can be corrected by better noun selection, and better ordering of the phrases, as illustrated in the revised paragraph, below.

Good: Mr. Bush and Mr. Sugihara both worked on two proposals, one that was originally developed by Mr. Sugihara as well as one sent from the head office. Mr. Bush wanted to add something to Mr. Sugihara's basic plan, and so he helped in developing the revisions. As a result the plan has since undergone major changes. It was a lot of work but both were pleased with the way Mr. Sugihara's plan turned out.

In the revised paragraph, above, we now know *which* plan was developed further, complete with major revisions, *who* wanted to add something to the original and *which* plan they were finally happy with. In longer paragraphs, Mr. Sugihara's name can be replaced with *he*, the *plan* with *it*, etc., after it is clear that we have focused on one subject, and not the other. Shorter paragraphs, however, require that we make clear distinctions both between multiple subjects, and, multiple objects.

Examples.

Bad: Ms. Yabe confronted her secretary, Mrs. Thornquist, with the problem. She denied that she had any responsibility in the affair, and asked that she no longer involve her in the matter.

Good: **Ms. Yabe confronted her secretary, Mrs. Thornquist, with the problem. Ms. Yabe denied that she had any responsibility in the affair, and asked that Mrs. Thornquist no longer involve her in the matter.**

Bad: The terms of the contract were first decided by the former company owner and the vice president of Cross-Pacific Enterprises. The contract called for the joint construction of a single fishing boat. They have since replaced their vice president, and the owner is now the chairman of the company. It needs to be replaced with something more in line with our current situation.

Good: **The terms of the contract were first decided by the former owner of Atlantic Boats and the vice president of Cross-Pacific Enterprises. The contract called for the joint construction of a single fishing boat. Cross-Pacific later replaced their vice president, and the former Atlantic Boats owner is now the chairman of Cross-Pacific. The old contract needs to be replaced with something more in line with our current situation.**

Bad: I am pleased to announce that ABM has come out with a new smart phone that has built in fax and e-mail capability. It is the first time that a smart phone has included both of these features in the base system. It is a feature that should appeal to consumers who don't want to deal with extra soft and hardware just to send messages.

Good: **I am pleased to announce that ABM has come out with a new smart phone that has built in fax and e-mail capability. It is the first time that a smart phone has included both of these features in the base system. The feature of e-mail readiness should appeal to consumers who don't want to deal with extra soft and hardware just to send messages.**

II. PRINCIPLE OF DIRECTNESS – C. PARAGRAPH LEVEL.
b. STATE THE SUBJECT CLEARLY

(46)   Focus on the Message by Placing the Writer in the Background.

This is a general rule of writing which focuses the reader's attention on *what* you say, not *how* you say it. Another way to state this rule is to simply *let the facts speak for themselves.* Notice that this is of course in clear contradiction to a text that is sprinkled with personal opinions, anecdotes and observations, all of which tend to thrust the writer into the forefront of the discussion. By placing yourself in the background, you neutralize the mood and temper of your writing, helping to create an unbiased and direct discussion of the relevant issues.

How do we place ourselves in the background? One easy way is to limit the use of personal pronouns that refer to ourselves in the text. So, avoid using *I, me, mine, myself* (and their plural counterparts). This may seem to contradict one of our earlier rules, *Use the first person singular active voice* (Rule #4, above), but in fact, does not. We still want to write in the first person singular active voice, we just don't need to call attention to ourselves in doing so. In some cases, when we repeatedly use *I*, for sentences beginning with *I think, I assume, I believe,* etc., we are introducing opinion structures that are usually not desirable. In other cases repeated use of *I* can cause the reader to feel that he or she is being talked down to, that the writer is placing himself above the reader. In this situation, using frequent personal references tend to *increase* the distance between the writer and the audience, rather than establish close rapport, though this is not the case of the *inclusive* first person plural pronouns, like *we*, which is used extensively throughout this text. If the first person plural pronouns such as *we* are used *exclusively*, however, this will create the same lack of rapport with your audience, since this usage tends to separate the writer (and his exclusive group) from the audience (unless it is clear the reader in included in *we*). So, instead of prefacing your statements with *I believe, I think, I see, it is clear to me, we have decided, from our point of view,* and so forth, just make the statements in a direct and straightforward way, with the writer in the background, and the focus on the content.

Examples.

Bad: I'd like to begin my memo with an announcement that the members of my staff in the research and development section have all given me a great deal of satisfaction by winning the annual Design Achievement Award, given out at the Mechanical Engineering Banquet which I attended last week in Miami.

Good: **I'd like to congratulate the members of the research and development staff for winning the annual Design Achievement Award, given out at the Mechanical Engineering Banquet which I attended last week in Miami.**
(or)

Good: **Congratulations to the members of the research and development staff for winning the annual Design Achievement Award, given out at the Mechanical Engineering Banquet which was held last week in Miami.**

Bad: I would like to suggest that if you all followed my example of getting to work on time, you would find that you would be able to get your work done on time, like I am.

Good: **I would like everyone to concentrate on getting to work on time, so that you are able to get your work done on time.**

Bad: It is clear to me that the nature of the problem lies in the way the ordering system is designed. If you follow my advice, just do what I do, and cut out the middle man.

Good: **The nature of the problem lies in the way the ordering system is designed, with the middle man an unnecessary element in the system.**

II. PRINCIPLE OF DIRECTNESS – C. PARAGRAPH LEVEL.
c. STATE THE "BOTTOM LINE" SUCCINCTLY

(47) Avoid Developing Ideas that you Intend to Dismiss Later.

It is rarely useful to discuss ideas that you intend to dismiss later. This is not the same thing as giving some attention to alternative solutions to problems that have been presented before offering what you consider the best solution. In technical writing, such as writing in the various sciences, it is common practice to begin by reviewing the ideas that others have proposed before presenting one's own unique approach. Usually, the writer starts with the most popular, or most common, ideas that are relevant to his discussion, and argues that for one reason or another, these ideas do not satisfactorily address his concerns. At each step, though, he discusses relevant issues, and then shows why they are not satisfactory. Finally, he presents his own solution, and shows how it answers all of the earlier questions, and a usually a few more as well. This form of argumentation is not only acceptable in many technical discussions, but expected.

It is best to avoid introducing obscure ideas and arguments just for the sole purpose of *being able* to dismiss them later in favor of your own proposal. There is a fine line that separates what constitutes a reasonable argument that is a good candidate for attack and dismissal, and a poor candidate. Generally, they must be relevant to the present discussion (some proposals are too dated, others simply do not refer to the same facts, still others are concerned with different aspects of the facts, etc.).

When you do have points that you feel necessary to include, and later argue against, let the audience know early on that you intend to show how these early lines of reasoning will be abandoned. Let the audience know from the beginning that you are considering certain points only to show how they are lacking in some area or another, rather than simply leading them along, so that they think they are reading proposals that you support. It is best to simply say that you will first consider alternative ideas related to your proposal, and show why they are not satisfactory, before going on to your own ideas, rather than to pretend that you accept these intermediate ideas fully.

> Examples.

Bad: I will now discuss the single unit hypothesis. It was the first hypothesis proposed to describe the prosodic system of Japanese, and is still employed by many Japanese linguists today (...explanation...). However, the single unit hypothesis is not compatible with modern generative theory. Instead, I propose a form of the dual unit hypothesis.

Good: **I will now discuss the dual unit hypothesis for Japanese prosodic structure. I will argue that this is clearly preferred to the single unit hypothesis (...explanation...).**

Bad: Since we no longer have a janitorial staff, we need to deal with garbage disposal. One solution to the waste management problem is to hold everyone responsible for their own garbage. In this plan, each employee is expected to take their own trash home with them when they leave at the end of the day. However, I prefer a solution that deals with the problem right here. A possible on-site solution to the waste management problem is to require everyone to bring their own garbage to the refuse recycling building themselves.

Good: **Since we no longer have a janitorial staff, we need to deal with garbage disposal. A possible solution to the waste management problem is to require everyone to bring their own garbage to the refuse recycling building.**

Bad: One way to distribute messages is to type up a single copy, make an offset master, and run off enough copies for everyone in the building. Then, send copies to the various departments for distribution. However, since we got an e-mail network, and everyone has computers, we can just type one message and send it everyone in one step.

Good: **We used to give everyone hard copies of memos. However, now that we have an e-mail network, and everyone has computers, we can just type one message and send it to everyone electronically in one step.**

II. PRINCIPLE OF DIRECTNESS – C. PARAGRAPH LEVEL.
d. AVOID NEGATIVES WHENEVER POSSIBLE

(48)   Avoid Spite and Sarcasm.

Writing with *spite* means that you are writing with ill intentions towards someone (or something). *Sarcasm*, on the other hand, usually refers to the idea of saying the opposite of what you really mean. Both spite and sarcasm should be avoided in writing at all times.

When people write with *spite*, they are usually writing in response to something that has enraged them, and they are writing to get back at the person(s) who caused the problem. Writing with spite is even worse than speaking with spite, though, since your words are on permanent record (on paper), and could at some point be used to work against you. This does not mean that you cannot criticize people or ideas, and that you cannot voice strong displeasure towards various people or ideas. Your words should never be used to injure anyone purposefully, but rather, to point out inadequacies in a constructive and positive manner. It is usually best to hold on to a memo that you have written in angry response to some situation for a few days, or at least long enough to have had time to reflect on the situation, and to have considered the issues in a calmer light. Then, reread your memo, and see if it is confrontational and/or inflammatory. If it is, throw it away, and write a more reasoned response.

Sarcasm, on the other hand, refers to saying something opposite to what you mean. While this is sometimes acceptable in spoken English (usually as a form of humor), on paper it is usually difficult to tell whether the person seriously believes the statement as it is written, or if he is being sarcastic, and actually means the opposite of what is stated. For example, a sarcastic comment like "From what I saw last week, your employees really don't like working for you," where what was intended to be a joke (the writer actually thought the employees loved their work), can be interpreted negatively, since the reader can see only what is on paper (which looks to be a statement of criticism of his employees). Because of the possibility of misunderstanding, sarcasm is to be avoided.

> Examples.

Bad: I have responded to your request for payment at least five times already, and each time the answer is the same. I have already paid off my bills in full and I have the receipts to show for it. If any of you idiots took the time to actually read one of the letters I sent you, you would see what a stupid mistake you have been making. Get off my back already.

Good: **The enclosed bill has already been paid in full. I have included a copy of my receipts. I ask that you correct your records on this as soon as possible.**

Bad: I feel that I was not given proper warning nor a fair hearing when I was reprimanded for allegedly behaving improperly towards an "unnamed" colleague. You may not know it but she drinks quite a bit, even on the job, and cannot in my opinion be trusted. I never did the things she must have said I did, and I never have done anything wrong. If you want to get somebody, why don't you get her?

Good: **I want to thank you for pointing out areas that I need improvement on, and ask for your patience as I attempt to work these problems out. I appreciate your concern, and will do my best to deal with the points you raised in our discussion.**

Bad: I would love to attend the reception for Citizens Against Beer Drinking.

Good: **I am not interested in attending the reception for Citizens Against Beer Drinking.**

Bad: I just wanted to let you know that I really appreciated the fact that you have been late for work nearly every day since you started working with us. It suggests to us that you enjoy your job and are happy to be part of our team.

Good: **I just wanted to let you that we are concerned about the fact that you have been late for work nearly every day since you started working with us. It suggests to us that you are not enjoying your job and are not happy to be part of our team. Please see me at once.**

II. PRINCIPLE OF DIRECTNESS – C. PARAGRAPH LEVEL.
d. AVOID NEGATIVES WHENEVER POSSIBLE

(49)   Be Direct, but Not Too Direct.

Sometimes we can be too direct, or too blunt, so here we will *focus on being direct, but not too direct.* Keep in mind that we want to make our readers comfortable and willing to read what we have written. Maintain the levels of distinction that exist in the office in your writing as well. It is inappropriate then, for the boss of a major corporation to write a memo to employees he has never met as if he were writing a letter to one of his close personal friends. Here, the most direct, familiar approach is not expected, and will seem awkward and contrived, as if the boss is pretending to be "one of the guys," where it is clear that he most definitely is not. By adopting a tone and style that is informal (but not overly personal) for most common correspondences, including memos to all different ranks of employees, you will work to bring the idea of community and business family closer together.

Memos of substance, however, require more care and control. These are memos that convey important news to others, often of an official nature. The news might be notification of promotion, acceptance, as well as layoffs, denials of appeals, and so forth. For good news, it is never too early to read it. You can start off a letter with "*congratulations*", and the excited reader will race to the good news. Bad news, however, usually requires a bit more tact, where the direct approach should be avoided. In other words, it is rarely suitable to tell someone that their contract is not being renewed by beginning with an opening line such as "*You're fired.*" That approach is too direct for most situations. However, it is useful to give the readers an indication that bad news is contained within by stating early in the memo something like "*It is with regrets that we inform you that (we are unable to renew your contract).*" While only slightly less direct than the "*You're fired*" approach, the less direct method is more desirable, though it is slightly more formal and, therefore, impersonal. Ultimately, discussing even bad news in a positive constructive manner is much easier on your readers than being overly direct, blunt, tactless and destructive.

Examples.

Bad: I reviewed your application and you have nothing to offer us. We are not interested in hiring you.

Good: **I reviewed your application and I regret to inform you that we have nothing to offer you at this time. I wish you the best of luck in your job search.**

Bad: Your shipment was lost at sea. Since you had no insurance you lost everything. Have a nice day.

Good: **We regret to inform you that your shipment was lost at sea. Unfortunately, you did not take out the insurance option, so we are unable to reimburse you for your loss. We greatly regret this situation, and hope that you will continue to honor us with your business.**

Bad: Your request for an extended leave of absence without pay has been denied.

Good: **I am sorry to say that at this time we are unable to grant your request for an extended leave of absence without pay. You may wish to inquire again when our schedule is not so busy.**

Bad: Well, boys and girls, once again it is time to cough up for our annual charity drive. Now, before you throw this memo away, let me say that I am counting on each and every one of you for making some kind contribution, so don't be caught with your pants down.

Good: **Once again it is time to contribute to our annual charity drive. Let me say that I am counting on each and every one of you for making some kind contribution, so please give some thought to a worthy cause.**

III. PRINCIPLE OF ECONOMY

Overview

The *Principle of Economy* contains four rules. These rules include:

1) Brief is best;
2) High frequency words are preferred over low frequency "specialty" words;
3) Avoid subordination, and;
4) Discuss one point per statement.

In essence, the Principle of Economy can be summarized as "brief is best." This principle helps to trim a text of unnecessary words, sentences and ideas, so that the point of focus is placed clearly on the key elements of the message. Many of these rules also are closely related to the Principle of Directness, since wordiness tends to obscure meaning and focus.

The first rule, **Brief is best** includes several guidelines. The first, *Using a few key words correctly is better than using a lot of words incorrectly*, suggests that it is best to use words that you are familiar with, that are clear to both you and your readers, and not to embellish your text with words that your only partly understand. There are times when we look to the dictionary for a suitable word, but unless you are quite certain that the word is an appropriate choice for your text, it is best to become more familiar with the word by using it in casual conversation first, before committing it to text. So, the rule here suggests that you stick with what you do know in your writing, so that you can write with ease and confidence. The second guideline of the **Brief is best** axiom, *Fewer words in a sentence are preferred to expanded or extended narratives*, again is very similar to the first, only the point here is that the basic length of sentences should be limited, rather than expanded, regardless of the issues of word familiarity and suitableness. Within a sentence, we sometimes refer two or three times to the same subject or object, where only one reference is necessary. Similarly, some things don't need to be stated, or restated, since it is obvious from the context what the thing is. At the paragraph level, this idea is expanded to suggest that *fewer sentences are preferred to expanded discourse*. Sometimes we find ourselves repeating points made in other ways elsewhere in the text. This rule suggests that we consider carefully whether such repetition is necessary. In general, if the message can be shortened and still convey the key elements, then the shortened form is best.

The second main rule, **High frequency words are preferred over low frequency "specialty" words**, is similar to the first rule, and differs only in the fact that though the specialized vocabulary may be familiar to you (which it is not in the first rule) it is still better to avoid the specialized terminology in favor of more common word choices. Of course, the Principle of Cohesiveness is also relevant here, since you need to choose a technical level suitable for your audience. However, for most general business communications, the vocabulary should lean more toward the common than the specialized, and effort should be taken to not introduce too many terms that are unfamiliar to your audience.

The third main rule, **Avoid subordination**, simply encourages the writer to not embed too many sentences within other sentences. We want to avoid putting too many dependent clauses within the same sentence, since it then becomes difficult to determine the main point of the statement.

The fourth main rule, **Discuss one point per statement**, is similar to the third; both rules in fact suggest that it is best to break up complex sentences into simpler and more manageable statements. By discussing one point per statement, it is easy for the reader to follow your line of reasoning in a straightforward manner, and understand clearly what you consider to be the key elements. When two or more points are merged into a single statement, the point of focus is often lost.

III. PRINCIPLE OF ECONOMY – A. WORD LEVEL.
a. BRIEF IS BEST: USING A FEW KEY WORDS CORRECTLY IS BETTER THAN USING A LOT OF WORDS INCORRECTLY

(50)   <u>Use Words You Know.</u>

This is a simple rule of Economy. Basically, it is best to use words that you understand clearly and are used to using, so that you can write with confidence and clarity. You are specifically discouraged from using words that you have seen or heard elsewhere, but have not become part of your normal vocabulary. It is best to test these words out in informal conversations before committing them to print. Often we are able to guess the meanings of unfamiliar words from the context in which they are used, but just as often we may in fact have not guessed correctly, or may have at least missed important nuances.

Similarly, when searching for an appropriate word, we may resort to a dictionary, a common practice for all writers. It is best, however, to use the dictionary to <u>check or confirm</u> your understanding of a given word, rather than to use it produce an entirely unknown word. This may sound somewhat strange, since it is usually the goal of all second language learners to acquire new vocabulary. In business and technical writing, however, it is best to leave your lessons behind and concentrate on developing clear ideas using words and structures that you know.

When unfamiliar words are taken straight out of the dictionary, they are often misused. The misuse could be a result of the writer not fully understanding all of the various nuances of meaning, or because it is a vulgar alternative to a more appropriate choice, or because the word requires a specific preposition to convey an intended meaning. In order to avoid choosing the wrong words, it is best to simply use words you know.

This doesn't mean that you should stop increasing your vocabulary. You are of course encouraged to expand and develop your understanding of the English language in all aspects. Instead, you are encouraged to limit the language that you commit to paper to the language that you know well, and can use correctly. Over time you will naturally expand the base of understanding, and the breadth of your vocabulary.

Examples.

Bad: The precipice of the container is made of plastic.

Good: The top of the container is made of plastic.

Bad: We hope to elicit enough funds to begin an employee owned credit union.

Good: We hope to raise enough funds to begin an employee owned credit union.

Bad: The new dispenser allows liquid to flow with fluidity.

Good: The new dispenser allows liquid to flow smoothly.

Bad: We no longer stock replacement parts for the contrivance that you have listed.

Good: We no longer stock replacement parts for the product that you have listed.

Bad: Please send us one specimen of your work, along with your resume.

Good: Please send us one example of your work, along with your resume.

Bad: The discovery by Dr. Suzuki was truly epoch-making in the field of Japanese anthropology.

Good: The discovery by Dr. Suzuki was truly revolutionary in the field of Japanese anthropology.

Bad: The sparkling white mountain precipice contrasted sharply with the deep blue sky.

Good: The sparkling white mountain peak contrasted sharply with the deep blue sky.

III. PRINCIPLE OF ECONOMY – A. WORD LEVEL.
b. COMMON WORDS ARE PREFERRED OVER UNCOMMON WORDS

(51)   Use Common Words Instead of Uncommon Specialty Words.

We have noted earlier that overly formal writing should be avoided in most business communications. One way the writing is made too formal is by using too many special low frequency (uncommon) words. Low frequency words are words that are not used very often, and as such, are likely to be unfamiliar to at least some of your audience. The use of uncommon specialty words tends to formalize a document, increasing the distance between the writer and the audience. In some documents, such as formal contracts, this distance is acceptable. However, for most business communications, some degree of familiarity is expected, so common words are preferred over uncommon words. So, instead of a sentence like "It may merit our scrutiny," we should write something like "It is worth looking into," or simply "We will look into it."

Continuing the theme of preferring common words to uncommon ones, the following word pairs suggest some of the possibilities.

Bad	Good	Bad	Good
acknowledge	admit	homogeneous	same, uniform
adjacent	next to	indicate	tell, show
antithesis	opposite	instantaneously	instantly
ascertain	find out	multifaceted	diverse
commence	start	notwithstanding	however
conversely	on the other hand	ramification	result
culminate	end, result in	recapitulate	repeat
embark	begin	scrutinize	look
finalize	finish	terminate	end, fire
heretofore	before	unequivocally	clearly

Not all uncommon words are special. Some, in fact, are used within a particular sub-group of the English-using population, but are not appropriate for mainstream writing, while others are simply vulgar. For example, stating that you don't like something by saying that you have bad *karma* about it is inappropriate: there are better and more precise words to use to indicate your displeasure. Similarly, while "*ain't*" is frequently heard in some dialects of English, it is still quite uncommon in professional writing, and as such, should be avoided. In general, if you haven't seen the word before in text, it is best to avoid it.

> Examples.

Bad: The ramifications of the new plan are far-reaching, everyone in the company will be affected.

Good: **The results of the new plan are far-reaching, everyone in the company will be affected.**

Bad: After you have read this letter, please take a moment to scrutinize the new health benefits proposal.

Good: **After you have read this letter, please take a moment to look over the new health benefits proposal.**

Bad: After you have finalized the corrections on the draft, please have Ms. Smith check it over.

Good: **After you have finished correcting the draft, please have Ms. Smith check it over.**

Bad: The new copier can switch from making black and white copies to color copies instantaneously.

Good: **The new copier can instantly switch from making black and white copies to color copies.**

Bad: Mr. Burton's position on the new proposal is the antithesis of ours.

Good: **Mr. Burton's position on the new proposal is the opposite of ours.**

Bad: So, if I may recapitulate the main points of the discussion, I think it is important to...

Good: **So, if I may repeat the main points of the discussion, I think it is important to...**

III. PRINCIPLE OF ECONOMY – A. WORD LEVEL.
b. COMMON WORDS ARE PREFERRED OVER UNCOMMON WORDS

(52)   <u>Define/Gloss Special, New and Unknown Terms, Acronyms, and Expressions.</u>

There are times when it is necessary to use uncommon words in our text, especially when we are discussing new technology, and new advances in our given professions. Even if the audience *should* be aware of the new terms, it is always best to define the new terms when they are first introduced in the text. Special, new and unknown terms may simply be words that already exist in the dictionary, but are not commonly used. They may be words that are normally used in different contexts, and as such, require an explanation as to how they will be used in a different way in your text. For example, if you use the term *play* to describe the amount of looseness in the fan belt of a car engine, though 'play' is a common word, its use as an indicator of "degree of looseness" is not very common, and should be defined in the new context of your text. Words that are relatively uncommon, such as 'autochthonous' (native to a specific area of land) should be defined unless it is clearly understood by all in your field of expertise. New words are usually a result of a new discovery, frequently related to science and industry. Computer terms such as 'hard disk', 'mouse' and 'software' have become commonly accepted terms only within the last twenty years or so, while other terms such as 'viral', 'blog' and 'text' (as a verb) may not be completely understood by everyone, and as such, might require definition if they are to be used in your text.

Acronyms, too, need to be defined at the point of their introduction into the text, except for the most common acronyms such as U.N. (for the United Nations). When in doubt as to whether the acronyms are widely understood, take the safe route and define them in the text. For example, while IBM® is understood in many places of the world, you still might want to begin with a gloss of what the acronym stands for (as in, "International Business Machines, hereafter referred to as IBM"), just to be sure that there is no misunderstanding. In most cases, it is not advisable to make up your own acronyms, especially for already existing organizations and companies. Finally, acronyms are not usually made from single words, so companies such as Sony® and Kodak® do not become "S" and "K," respectively.

Examples.

Bad: We have entered into a new partnership with International Plastics. International Plastics will handle all of our domestic operations.

Good: **We have entered into a new partnership with International Plastics (hereafter referred to as IP). IP will handle all of our domestic operations.**

Bad: The most interesting feature of the new IP personal computers is the virtual memory capability. This feature is unique to the IP computers.

Good: **The most interesting feature of the new IP personal computers is the virtual memory capability. Virtual memory refers to the ability to store information separately, and can be referred to even if it has not been saved. This feature is unique to the IP computers.**

Bad: The windage factor is critical in the design of fuel efficient automobiles.

Good: **The windage factor (the factor related to the effect that wind has on an object) is critical in the design of fuel efficient automobiles.**

Bad: Mo-Par has developed a new line of cleaning products.

Good: **Mo-Par (formerly More Power Products) has developed a new line of cleaning products.**

Bad: Yanosonic (hereafter referred to as Y) announced today that they would no longer be handling repairs for appliances over ten years old. A spokesman for Y...

Good: **Yanosonic announced today that they would no longer be handling repairs for appliances over ten years old. A spokesman for Yanosonic...**

III. PRINCIPLE OF ECONOMY – A. WORD LEVEL.
b. COMMON WORDS ARE PREFERRED OVER UNCOMMON WORDS

(53)   Avoid Coining New Words and Phrases.

Whenever possible, use already existing words and phrases in your writing. However, since many of our fields are advancing at a rate faster than current vocabulary can adequately handle, we are sometimes tempted to create our own words and expressions to describe these new developments. For the most part, though, there likely is an existing word, or a possible phrase, that can handle most any new development. These possibilities should be thoroughly explored before introducing new terms to an already extensive English vocabulary. The problem with the introduction of terms that we have created ourselves is whether they will be understood by anyone else. Many car, stereo and computer manufacturers ignore this concern, and constantly advertise their products with features described in unique terms that only the manufacturers themselves seem to understand. There is little value in this approach, in that no one really puts much effort into trying to understand what an 'attenuator' ("a device used to reduce force") really is, much less whether they need one in their audio system or not. Often manufacturers have assumed that the more fancy words that are used, the more advanced (and therefore attractive) their product will appear.

While the high tech industry is constantly coming up with new terms, mostly to entice the public, newspapers and mass media are coining their own terms, usually as a means of shortening text (or speech) that becomes difficult to reproduce in their various media formats. "*High-tech*" itself is such a shortened form, based on the expression *high technology,* just as "*hi-fi*" was developed from *high fidelity* some fifty or sixty years ago.

Though it is advisable not to create new words, there are situations when no existing terms are appropriate. In this case, your new coinages should be based upon the existing rules of the language (where, for example, **lfpug* is not permissible, but *elfplug* is), and usually should simply be a word (or phrase) made up of already existing words (such as: *elf + plug*).

> Examples.

Bad: The new air conditioner features softair capabilities.

Good: The new air conditioner creates a gentle breeze.

Bad: The sharp-o-matic does the job in half the time of conventional units.

Good: The sharpener does the job in half the time of conventional units.

Bad: This week we plan to featurette the new health meal.

Good: This week we plan to feature the new health meal.

Bad: The new drug is for people who find themselves coming home tiredly everyday after work.

Good: The new drug is for people who find themselves coming home tired everyday after work.

Bad: The new cavnel connects the gift shop to the viewing deck.

Good: The new cave tunnel connects the gift shop to the viewing deck.

Bad: The outdoor adventure gear collection includes a survival kit, binoculars, canteen and a band-o-leer.

Good: The outdoor adventure gear collection includes a survival kit, binoculars, canteen and an over-the-shoulder-belt for carrying everything.

Bad: They have called the new candy "plnpeel."

Good: They have called the new candy "pull-n-peel."

III. PRINCIPLE OF ECONOMY – B. SENTENCE LEVEL.
a. BRIEF IS BEST: FEWER WORDS IN A SENTENCE ARE PREFERRED TO EXPANDED OR EXTENDED NARRATIVES

(54)   Restrict Length of Sentences.

For the sake of economy and clarity, the length of sentences should be restricted, especially when multiple subjects and/or multiple objects are involved. One way to restrict sentence length is to limit each sentence to the discussion of one point. Another is to break sentences up when it is not clear whether the comment is about the subject or the object. Still another way is to count the number of conjunctions in your sentence; if there are more than one or two, then the sentence is likely too long. Finally, if there is more than one dependent clause in a sentence, the sentence is likely quite complex, and more than likely, too long.

Often, the <u>outline system suitable for paragraph organization has been utilized inappropriately *within* a sentence.</u> For example, the *chronological* system of outlining, which considers events in the temporal order in which they occurred, can lead to overly long sentences when employed within a sentence: *"ABM first started out as a computer accessory manufacturer, *then* it acquired the Kansas City production facility, *and later* it was able to produce its own line of small personal computers, *after which* it entered into the business sector of computer production." This last sentence has too many conjunctions, contains too many points, and covers too much ground to be considered a good sentence. Other systems of paragraph outlining can be similarly abused.

The worst kinds of errors are often the simplest. Very long sentences that are simply strings of shorter sentences connected by *and, and then, next,* etc. are particularly awkward: *"I arrived at the convention site *and* I went to the exhibition hall *and* I met with the supervisor *and* he told me I was too late to register *and* he suggested that I go to second exhibition hall." Remember, though, that too many simple sentences are just as unpleasant as too many overly long sentences. In general, one or two simple related ideas in a single sentence is fine, but no more than one complex idea.

Examples.

Bad: First, I would like to inquire about prices for various printing supplies (see the enclosed list), and also, I am interested in getting information about the new colored binders, and I want to find out when your color printers will be operating.

Good: **I would like some information about prices and other things. First, I need prices for various printing supplies (see the enclosed list). Also, I am interested in getting information about the new colored binders. Finally, I would like to know when your color printers will be operating.**

Bad: Please send us three reams of letter sized heavy bond typing paper, and order a new Dec 3900 personal computer, and check on the availability of the double capacity ink cartridges.

Good: **Please send us three reams of letter sized heavy bond typing paper. Also, I would like to order a new Dec 3900 personal computer. Finally, please check on the availability of the double capacity ink cartridges.**

Bad: In this report I discuss last year's sales figures, and our expectations for this year's sales, and I will talk about some changes we are thinking of to increase sales in the future, and I will also discuss the possibility of expanding our operations into other market areas.

Good: **In this report I discuss several items. I begin by reviewing last year's sales figures, and then comment on our expectations for this year's sales. I will then talk about some changes we are thinking of to increase sales in the future, and I will conclude by discussing the possibility of expanding our operations into other market areas.**

III. PRINCIPLE OF ECONOMY – B. SENTENCE LEVEL.
a. BRIEF IS BEST: FEWER WORDS IN A SENTENCE ARE PREFERRED TO EXPANDED OR EXTENDED NARRATIVES

(55)   <u>Keep Sentences Separate in Ambiguous Situations.</u>

Often sentences are made unclear, or ambiguous, because they lack appropriate conjunctions. In other situations, sentences are unclear, as demonstrated elsewhere, because of the possible confusion over multiple subjects and objects. In this discussion, we will look at the problems caused by not having conjunctions where they should be. The remedy is of course to use appropriate conjunctions to separate (or to at least signal a disjuncture) between two clauses, or sentences. Frequently, though, it is better just to break the sentence into two separate units. Remember that some conjunctions, such as *though, while* and *even if* do not have to be placed between two sentences, but may be used at the beginning of a complex sentence.

Sometimes we try to separate two ideas contained within a single sentence by simply inserting a comma between the two ideas: *"The crew worked throughout the night, this morning they did not finish until late." This sentence is awkward, however, and can be improved upon, either by adding a conjunction or by separating it into two complete separate sentences: "Though the crew worked throughout the night, they did not finish until late this morning," or; "The crew worked throughout the night. Unfortunately, they did not finish until late this morning."

Other sentences are ambiguous despite the inclusion of conjunctions because it is unclear whether the subject or the object is involved in the comment. In these ambiguous sentences, it is best to simply break the idea up into separate sentences. In the sentence *"The president and his personal assistant both visited the new facility, and he was impressed with the operations," it is unclear whether the president or the assistant was the one who was impressed. We need to break the message up: "The president and his personal assistant both visited the new facility. The president was impressed with the operations."

> Examples.

Bad: Type up the minutes to last Friday's meeting, put it in my box when you are done.

Good: **Type up the minutes to last Friday's meeting and put a copy in my box when you are done.**
(or)
Good: **When you have finished typing up the minutes to last Friday's meeting put a copy in my box when you are done.**
(or)
Good: **Type up the minutes to last Friday's meeting. When you have finished, put a copy in my box.**

Bad: I am writing to thank you for inviting us to your end-of-year party, for our entire staff.

Good: **I am writing to thank you for inviting us to your end-of-year party, and to thank you for inviting our entire staff.**
(or)
Good: **I am writing to thank you for inviting our entire staff to your end-of-year party.**
(or)
Good: **I am writing to thank you for inviting us to your end-of-year party. I am particularly grateful that you extended the invitation to our entire staff.**

Bad: The supervisor talked to her secretary for nearly an hour, then she left immediately for lunch.

Good: **After talking to her secretary for nearly an hour, the supervisor left immediately for lunch.**

III. PRINCIPLE OF ECONOMY – B. SENTENCE LEVEL.
a. BRIEF IS BEST: FEWER WORDS IN A SENTENCE ARE PREFERRED TO EXPANDED OR EXTENDED NARRATIVES

(56)   Avoid Restatement and Redundancy.

Restatement and redundancy can occur in many forms. At the sentence level, redundancy often comes from the unnecessary repetition of identical words, or of words referring to the same idea. While repetition is not to be avoided altogether, (it is a means for emphasizing points and is often used in summaries or conclusions), here, we focus on the problem of redundancy caused by unnecessary repetition of words, or repeated reference to the same idea.

The most common error of repetition is to state the subject twice, as in "The *boss, he* is being transferred to Tokyo." In this example, either *he* or the *boss* is not necessary (*boss* must already have been mentioned in order to delete "boss" from the sentence, however).

Another type of redundancy is caused by using two or more words which *overlap* in meaning: "*This* plan *here* is good." Both *this* and *here* refer to something <u>near</u> the speaker, and if *this* is used, then *here* is not necessary. Similarly, some words just don't need to be put together: "It is a modern new building," seems harmless enough, but can we say "It is a modern old building"? No, we can't, and for the same reason that the *modern new* building is odd as well: both *modern* and *new* contain *time* references (as does *old*), and to an extent, repeat the idea unnecessarily. For another example, in the sentence, "I am *currently teaching* at Edmonds Vocational Institute," the present progressive form of the verb (*verb + ing*) indicates the current state of affairs (i.e. what you are doing now), and by adding *currently*, you add an unnecessary extra word. Similarly, stores often offer *free gifts* to customers, but have you ever heard of a gift that you had to pay for?

Additionally, some things either *are*, or they *aren't*, but some writers won't leave absolutes alone, and feel that by adding an unnecessary word of qualification, the judgment will be even *more* absolute. For example, is something that is *completely true* more true that something that is *true*? Similarly, *foreign imports* can be simplified to *imports, personal opinion* to *opinion*, and so forth.

Finally, some terms are no longer needed because of redundancy through familiarity and usage. So, what was once a *gas automobile*, became just an *automobile*, and now simply an *auto* (or even simpler, a *car*). Similarly, an *electric* typewriter used to distinguish it from a (*manual*) typewriter, but quickly reverted back to *typewriter* as the need to distinguish between the two was no longer necessary (one replaced the other). Along these same lines, we would rarely write *electronic* computer, since the word *computer* implies electrical operation, in this day and age at least.

Examples.

Bad: I would like to introduce you to a new product which we have recently developed.
Good: **I would like to introduce you to an interesting product which we have recently developed.**

Bad: This model that you see here before you is our latest design.
Good: **This model is our latest design.**

Bad: Recently I have been working at ABM since May 2012.
Good: **I have been working at ABM since May 2012.**

Bad: The boss, he is being transferred to Tokyo.
Good: **The boss is being transferred to Tokyo.**

Bad: This plan here is good.
Good: **This plan is good.**

Bad: I am currently teaching at Edmonds Vocational Institute.
Good: **I am currently at Edmonds Vocational Institute.**
(or)
Good: **I am teaching at Edmonds Vocational Institute.**

Bad: It is a modern new building.
Good: **It is a new building.**
(or)
Good: **It is a modern building.**

III. PRINCIPLE OF ECONOMY – B. SENTENCE LEVEL.
a. BRIEF IS BEST: FEWER WORDS IN A SENTENCE ARE PREFERRED TO EXPANDED OR EXTENDED NARRATIVES

(57)   <u>Avoid Wordiness (replace wordy phrases with precise terms).</u>

This rule suggests that we should use the shortest sequence of words necessary to get our point across. Here we will focus on replacing wordy phrases with more precise terms and expressions. Just as uncommon specialty words tend to formalize our writing (see Rule #51), use of wordy phrases also tend to make our writing more dense and less accessible. Here, we are concerned with getting rid of a string of (usually) common words in favor of more precise and economical terms.

Phrases that include *manner, way, fact, method, purpose, reason* and related words often get encumbered with too many qualifying terms. For example, "the company should act in *a cautious manner*..." should be rewritten as "the company should act *cautiously*...". Similarly, in the sentence beginning "We need to secure finances for *the purpose of the* new plant..." should be rewritten as "We need to get finances *for* the new plant...". Also, "*The fact that* the deal fell through was cause for concern..." should be rewritten as simply "The deal falling through was cause for concern...". Below are a list of unnecessarily wordy expressions, and their more economical alternatives.

<u>Bad</u>	<u>Good</u>
(a check) in the amount of	**(a check) for**
are provided in	**are in**
at this point in time	**(now)**
did not succeed	**failed**
due to the fact that	**since, because**
I'd like to (request...)	**I (request...)**
in a brisk way	**quickly**
in a professional manner	**rofessionally**
in the event that	**if**
in the near future	**soon**
it has come to our attention that your...	**your....**
looking for something in the neighborhood of...	**looking for...**
unaware of the fact that	**unaware that**

The list above is merely suggestive of the kinds of wordiness that can occur, and some of the possible more economical alternative expressions. In general, remember, "brief is best."

> Examples.

Bad: We expect all of our employees to conduct themselves in a professional manner at all times.
Good: **We expect all of our employees to conduct themselves professionally at all times.**

Bad: It has come to our attention that your account is in remiss.
Good: **Your account is overdrawn.**

Bad: Due to the fact that we no longer manufacture that product, we are unable to provide spare parts.
Good: **Since we no longer manufacture that product, we are unable to provide spare parts.**

Bad: A new employee should act in a cautious manner when working with new equipment.
Good: **A new employee should act cautiously when working with new equipment.**
(or)
Good: **A new employee should use caution when working with new equipment.**

Bad: We need to secure finances for the purpose of building the new research facility.
Good: **We need to get finances for building the new research facility.**

Bad: The fact that the deal fell through was cause for concern for everyone.
Good: **Everyone was concerned about the deal falling through.**

III. PRINCIPLE OF ECONOMY – B. SENTENCE LEVEL.
a. BRIEF IS BEST: FEWER WORDS IN A SENTENCE ARE PREFERRED TO EXPANDED OR EXTENDED NARRATIVES

(58)   Use Mainly Nouns and Verbs.

This rule takes us back to an earlier rule (Rule #5), encouraging us to use basic "subject-verb-object" word order for sentences, where this structure outlined the basic components of the sentence. Here we build on this rule by suggesting that it is best to stay close to this S-V-O structure, and not to distract the reader from the main points of your text by adding in too many additional words that serve to qualify and describe the main words of the sentence. The nouns and the verbs are the things that anchor the message in reality, while the adjectives and adverbs simply put these things in different lights. It is best not to get too distracted by letting the qualifying words take over for the main elements of the sentence.

Using mainly nouns and verbs is a rule that is more relevant to good business writing than to writing other forms of communication, such as poetry and novels. In poetry, for example, it is often the colorful and creative imagery that is developed by unique juxtaposition of adjectives and adverbs that serve to form a vision that is distinct from all other visions. In business and technical applications, however, the writer is more often concerned with ensuring that all members of the audience read a text and essentially all come to the *same understanding* of it, rather than the readers of literature and poetry who may all read the same text and yet come away with very different understandings of the material. In order to help the readers all understand the same thing in professional applications, then, it is best to use concrete language, in a straightforward style, relying mainly on accurate usage of key nouns and verbs. This is of course not to say that adjectives and adverbs should be abandoned altogether. Rather, as a *principle* of Economy, it is a rule that provides *guidelines* for language usage, not *prohibitions*. In the next rule, then, we will discuss when and how to use adjectives and adverbs effectively. For our purposes here, however, it is suggested that we rely more on the power of concrete nouns and verbs in business and technical writing in order to convey our ideas plainly and clearly.

> Examples.

Bad: The extremely well designed engine is a fine example of Japanese technology at its best.

Good: The engine design is an example of Japanese technology at its best.

Bad: Our firm is renowned for its superb quality, excellent technique, and fantastic style.

Good: Our firm is known for its excellent quality, technique and style.

Bad: The reception was really very nice.

Good: The reception was very nice.

Bad: Quickly we need to efficiently work accurately.

Good: We need to work quickly and efficiently.

Bad: Effortlessly the special high powered air conditioner can quickly cool any room, large or small.

Good: The new high powered air conditioner can quickly cool any room, large or small.

Bad: I would like to order some inexpensive cheap perfume.

Good: I would like to order some inexpensive perfume.

Bad: The revolutionary medical practice will make extraordinarily miraculous changes in the field of cancer therapy.

Good: The revolutionary medical practice likely will create extraordinary changes in the field of cancer therapy.

III. PRINCIPLE OF ECONOMY – B. SENTENCE LEVEL.
a. BRIEF IS BEST: FEWER WORDS IN A SENTENCE ARE PREFERRED TO EXPANDED OR EXTENDED NARRATIVES

(59)   Avoid Overuse and Misuse of Adjectives.

We want to avoid using too many modifiers, such as adjectives and adverbs, so that the readers will not be distracted from the main message. However, sometimes they are necessary so we suggest that you use modifiers in "moderation." Whenever possible, modify nouns with at most only one adjective. Besides restricting the number of adjectives which modify a particular noun, there is also a natural order, or sequence, which you must employ when you use more than one adjective at a time. In this discussion, then, we will look at the proper sequencing of adjectives--remember, however, that the basic rule of Plain English is simply to avoid the ordering problem by using only a single adjective.

For those situations where more than one adjective is required to modify a noun, the general order of placement of some of the more common adjectives is as follows:

size --> age --> color --> origin --> material --> NOUN

The first important point is that adjectives are placed before the noun they modify. The second point is that you would not normally have more than two or three adjectives in any given sequence (each "slot" does not need to be filled), so the ordering is simply relative to those slots that are filled. Turning now to a few comments on each of the types of adjectives, "size" includes words like *big, small, tall, fat*; "age" includes *young, old, new, three-year old*; "color" (having to do with looks, and appearance) includes *red, dark, gloomy, dusty*; "origin" (having to do with type and source) includes *Chinese, Elizabethan, exotic*; and "material" (what something is made of) includes *brick, lace, metal*, and so forth.

Sometimes, when three or more adjectives are used in a description, slight differences of order are possible, such as *red brick Victorian* building, instead of *red Victorian brick* building. The best rule here is to avoid so many adjectives to modify just one noun, but if you can't, then you must realize that some words are more closely tied to each other than others (such as *red brick, yellow sandstone, black plastic* as modifiers), and these tight relationships must be retained.

Also concerning adjectives, when adjectives are placed in phrases with multiple subjects, the scope of affect can be misleading (see the related Rule

#39, above).

Bad: In the U.S., many old men and women live alone.

In the last example, *many* and *old* clearly modify *men*, but do they also both modify *women*?

In other words, the sentence could mean that *all women, and many old men live alone*, or, alternatively, *many old men and many women live alone*, or, finally, *many old men and many old women live alone*. We can ease the confusion by either repeating the adjectives before each noun (*many old men and many old women*), or, by rephrasing, such as *many old people*.

Examples.

Bad: Our office is located in a red old small Victorian brick building.
Good: Our office is located in small old red brick Victorian building.

Bad: Connect the blue thin wire to the brass small post.
Good: Connect the thin blue wire to the small brass post.

Bad: The high-pitched long siren goes off whenever the temperature in the furnace is too high.
Good: The long high-pitched siren goes off whenever the temperature in the furnace is too high.

Bad: Everyone is expected to dress in formal attire; for men, that means black long coats with tails....
Good: Everyone is expected to dress in formal attire; for men, that means long black coats with tails....

Bad: The new fax machine is housed in a sleek small black plastic case.
Good: The new fax machine is housed in a small black plastic case.

Bad: The house is furnished with antique rattan Chinese furniture.
Good: The house is furnished with antique Chinese rattan furniture.

III. PRINCIPLE OF ECONOMY – B. SENTENCE LEVEL.
a. BRIEF IS BEST: FEWER WORDS IN A SENTENCE ARE PREFERRED TO EXPANDED OR EXTENDED NARRATIVES

(60) Avoid Overuse and Misuse of Adverbs.

We want to avoid using too many modifiers, such as adjectives and adverbs. However, sometimes they are necessary so we suggest that you use modifiers in "moderation." Whenever possible, modify verbs with at most only one adverb. An exception to this rule is the use of adverbial phrases, which are composed of more than one word. (See related discussions on adverbial phrases and adverbs in Rules #38 & 39, above.)

Some adverbs are simply not necessary. These include *pretty, very, rather, little, really, fairly, nearly* and so forth. A sentence like "We need to *pretty much* be careful about our expenses for the next quarter," can be improved by deleting the modifiers (*pretty much*): "We need to be careful about our expenses for the next quarter." Sometimes two words can be replaced by one, as in "Bob *very nearly* set the records in sales last year," which can be rewritten as "Bob *almost* set the records in sales last year."

While one modifier may be necessary, two (or three) may confuse the reader. For example, "The company began a completely and utterly new course of development." Here, "*utterly*" is not necessary (it is redundant and distracting), and possibly "*completely*" is not necessary as well, (Is *completely new* different than *new*?). The following is more economical: "The company began a new course of development."

While two or three adjectives may sometimes be permissible (e.g., the *dirty old* building), it is rarely possible to combine two or more adverbs of *frequency* (adverbs that answer the question *how often*?) together to modify the same verb. So, in the next sentence, one adverb must be deleted: *"He often always works late," (we need to delete either *often* or *always*). Also, when we have two adverbs of manner (adverbs which answer the question *how*?), it is best to avoid using two adverbs to modify the same verb: *"He works quickly carefully." For this last example, we can insert *and* to correct the sentence *(He works quickly and carefully)*, or again, we can simply delete one of the adverbs *(He works carefully)*.

> Examples.

Bad: We expect that we will have to lay off fairly many of our most recently hired employees.

Good: We expect that we will have to lay off many of our most recently hired employees.

Bad: It is pretty hard to please both the management and the on-line staff at the same time.

Good: It is difficult to please both the management and the on-line staff at the same time.

Bad: The transformer is a completely brand-new design.

Good: The transformer is a brand-new design.

Bad: He often always works late.

Good: He often works late.

Bad: The weather forecaster predicted a fairly wet summer.

Good: The weather forecaster predicted a wet summer.

Bad: Sometimes he occasionally misses his appointments due to his drinking.

Good: He occasionally misses his appointments due to his drinking.

III. PRINCIPLE OF ECONOMY – B. SENTENCE LEVEL.
b. AVOID SUBORDINATE CLAUSES

(61)   Avoid Reported Speech.

Reported speech is the kind of statement that is made when a writer is citing facts or opinions that someone else has made. In informal writing, reported speech includes statements introduced by "he said," "Ms. Suzuki noted," and "the management has informed us that," etc. These phrases are followed by a paraphrase of the general message, and are not usually literal word-for-word transcriptions of the original statement. In more formal texts, though, it is often necessary to quote directly the original statement word-for-word.

It is best to begin with the basic rule of simply avoiding reported speech whenever possible. Reported speech is awkward, especially when the source is not quoted word-for-word, because it is often unclear where the writer's opinion leaves off, and the quoted source's opinion starts up. It is often very easy to confuse the borders between the writer and the source.

If reported speech must be included in the text, but is not directly quoted, then use phrases such as "*he reports that...*" "*Ms. Suzuki claims that...*" and follow this with a word-for-word account of the source's statement, changing only what is absolutely necessary. For example, the direct quote such as, *He stated "I am anxious to begin the new project as soon as possible"* can be changed to an indirect quote, as in, *He stated that he was anxious to begin the new project as soon as possible.* Note that the tense of the verb "*am*" in the direct quote is changed to "*was*" in the indirect quote. The trickiest part of using reported speech, and one of the reasons to try to avoid the form, is in determining which tense of the reported verb to use. Generally, if the reported statement was either made in the past (he *stated*), or about a past event, then the reported verb should be in the past as well. For another example, a direct quote such as *Ms. Suzuki states "I will do everything I can to improve working conditions"* must be changed into an indirect quote in the following way, *Ms. Suzuki states that she will do everything she can to improve working conditions."*

> Examples.

Bad: They said that we will have to cut several positions out of the current staff.

Good: **The Monbusho said that we would have to cut several positions out of the current staff.**

Bad: Ms. Suzuki claimed something to the effect that she was no longer interested in doing business with the bank consortium.

Good: **Ms. Suzuki stated that she was no longer interested in doing business with the bank consortium.**

Bad: Mr. Clark states that I can no longer trust them with our money.

Good: **Mr. Clark states "I can no longer trust them with our money."**
(or)
Good: **Mr. Clark states that he can no longer trust them with our money.**

Bad: The book, The Sound Pattern of English, says that there are five different major classes of consonants in English.

Good: **According to the book, The Sound Pattern of English, there are five different major classes of consonants in English.**

Bad: He told us to forget the disturbance and concentrate on meeting the deadline.

Good: **The supervisor told us to forget the disturbance and concentrate on meeting the deadline.**

Bad: Dr. Lee stated under no circumstances should the patient be moved.

Good: **Dr. Lee stated that under no circumstances should the patient be moved.**

III. PRINCIPLE OF ECONOMY – B. SENTENCE LEVEL.
b. AVOID SUBORDINATE CLAUSES

(62)   Using Subordinate Conjunctions (who, which, & what).

When we place one sentence within another, we often subordinate one of the sentences to the other. However, the end result is that the text is often rendered unnecessarily confusing. Therefore, whenever possible, it is best to simply avoid embedding one sentence within another. We cannot avoid these structures completely however, so on this page we review the best ways to use subordination, if you must use the structure.

The subordinate conjunction (*who, which* and *that*) is often placed in a dual role of both a conjunction *and* a subject reference. So, in *He is responsible for cleaning the offices, which he finds unchallenging, which* merely links a dependent (subordinate) clause to an independent one. However, in the next sentence, *which* also plays the role of a subject reference (referring to the act of *cleaning the offices*): *He is responsible for cleaning the offices, which is unchallenging for him.*

Another feature of the subordinators is that they can be either singular or plural, which can confuse the writer when she is trying to match tense and subject number: *I ate the grapes which I bought at the store,* and, *I ate the apple which I bought at the store.*

Using *who* is fairly straightforward. It is used to refer to people (singular or plural) and for nothing else. *She is the woman who is responsible for all personnel decisions,* and *They are the people who are responsible for all personnel decisions.* The tricky area here is using *who* in *object* reference, rather than subject. We have stated elsewhere that it is best just to simply avoid these passive structures altogether, but if employed, you must use the subordinator *whom,* instead of *who*: *The new employee with whom I spoke to earlier has great potential.* In the active voice, this sentence is much more straightforward: *I spoke earlier to a new employee who has great potential.*

Using *which* is similar to using *who,* above, except that we use this subordinator for anything that does not refer to people. *Which* has no alternate form for the passive voice, so its usage is even more straightforward than *who.* In some dialects, *which* is used to narrow focus, or explain, as in *The report, which was written by the president, is on the desk.* (adds information about the subject).

Finally, the easiest subordinator to use is *that.* It can be used in all places that either *who* or *which* can be used. In other words, *that* is a subordinator which can be used for *both* people-related subjects *and* non people-related subjects. So, if you want the simplest way to handle subordination, just use the subordinator *that*. However, as pointed out elsewhere, other considerations such as repetitiveness may warrant use of the other forms as well. In some dialects, *that* is used as an identifier, as in: *The report <u>that</u> the president wrote is on the desk* (tells us <u>which</u> report).

Examples.

Bad: Ms. Suzuki is the person which is in charge of import operations.
Good: **Ms. Suzuki is the person who is in charge of import operations.**
       (or)
Good: **Ms. Suzuki is the person that is in charge of import operations.**
Best: **Ms. Suzuki is in charge of import operations.**

Bad: Be sure to buy the on sale envelopes.
Good: **Be sure to buy the envelopes which are on sale.**
       (or)
Good: **Be sure to buy the envelopes that are on sale.**

Bad: The person to who I gave my resumé to no longer works for the company.
Good: **The person to whom I gave my resumé no longer works for the company.**

Bad: Please use the envelopes I gave you this morning for the letters you are typing now.
Good: **Please use the envelopes which I gave you this morning for the letters you are typing now.**
       (or)
Good: **Please use the envelopes that I gave you this morning for the letters you are typing now.**

Bad: Mr. Johnson heads a department he is not interested in running.
Good: **Mr. Johnson heads a department which he is not interested in running.**

III. PRINCIPLE OF ECONOMY – B. SENTENCE LEVEL.
a. AVOID SUBORDINATE CLAUSES

(63)   Using When and While as Conjunctions.

The use of the two conjunctions *when* and *while* is often misunderstood. One reason for the confusion is that both conjunctions refer to *time*, and both involve an idea of the passage or duration of time. Another source of confusion is that *while* also has other uses in English, and can sometimes be substituted in expressions normally using *and, but* and *although*. I suggest that you not use *while* as a replacement of *and, but* or *although* in all situations where substitution is possible. So, avoid the first example in favor of the second one, below.

Bad: While I understand his position, I cannot afford to take the risk.
Good: Although I understand his position, I cannot afford to take the risk.

Now, considering the differences between *when* and *while*, let us first look at how *while* is used. *While* is used when one action occurred in the midst of another action. Both actions are independent clauses, where one action lasts longer than the other. The longer of the two actions is modified by *while*, the shorter of the two actions is what occurred during the clause modified by *while*. *While*, then, is used to link two or more sentences made up of independent sentences into a single *compound* sentence. As such, *while* is a *coordinate* conjunction. So, for example: *While I was working at home, the phone rang.* The key here is that the action modified by *while* was in progress at the point in time that the other action occurred. In other words, the shorter action occurred during the time that the longer action was taking place.

When, on the other hand, is used to describe the point in time that some action took place. The point in time may in fact refer to another (longer) action, or may refer to an event. *When* is used to link a dependent clause to an independent clause, producing a *complex* sentence. *When*, then, is a *subordinate* conjunction (like *that, which* and *who*). For example:

When you contacted our office we were closed for our annual inventory.
We will introduce the new products *when* we sell off our current inventory.
When I understand what they are really offering, I will make a decision.
Please visit our factory *when* you have a chance.

For all of the last examples, *when* is used to modify either a clause that refers to a specific point in time, or the realization of a specific event. Another key difference between *when* and *while* should be obvious: *while* requires either the progressive, or the perfect, form of a verb in the clause that it is modifying, but *when* cannot be used to modify these verb forms. Of course this basic distinction is lost if we use *while* to substitute for *but*, *and* or *although*, discussed above. This is yet another reason to avoid this use of *while*, thereby allowing an easy distinction between *when* and *while*.

> Examples.

Bad: When you were on vacation, your deal fell through.
Good: While you were on vacation, your deal fell through.

Bad: While you may be correct, I still do not want to order a van.
Good: You may be correct, but I still do not want to order a van.

Bad: While we opened the box, the entire contents were discovered missing.
Good: When we opened the box, the entire contents were discovered missing.

Bad: We plan to take inventory while we close down over the New Year's break.
Good: We plan to take inventory when we close down over the New Year's break.

Bad: We plan to take inventory when we are closed over the New Year's break.
Good: We plan to take inventory while we are closed over the New Year's break.

Bad: If you meet Mr. Foster for the first time, you might think he is cold, but once you get to know him, you will find he is a very warm and sincere person.
Good: When you meet Mr. Foster for the first time, you might think he is cold, but once you get to know him, you will find he is a very warm and sincere person.

III. PRINCIPLE OF ECONOMY – B. SENTENCE LEVEL.
b. DISCUSS ONE POINT PER STATEMENT

(64)   Avoid Run-on Sentences.

Run-on sentences are sentences that contain two or more sentences (independent clauses), but do not contain appropriate coordinate conjunctions. These structures are called run-on sentences because one complete sentence does not terminate at a period, but rather, runs on into a second complete sentence. Recalling that the basic sentence structure of English is S-V-O, a run-on sentence has a basic structure of S-V-O-S-V-O (remember of course that not all sentences must have objects, and that S-V-O is simply the basic *representative* pattern). Sentences are run-on when they have at least this double basic sentence structure, and they don't have a conjunction linking one sentence to the other, or when they aren't separated by a semi-colon.

Correct Sentence Combination Formulas
1. S-V-O conjunction S-V-O
2. conjunction S-V-O, S-V-O
3. S-V-O; S-V-O

One of the common errors that result in run on sentences is the use of a comma instead of a semi-colon to separate the two sentences for the structure illustrated in #3, above. Though we will discuss the use of the semi-colon in more detail in a third section of this text, it is worth pointing out here that the semi-colon is used as a silent, or, non-lexical, conjunction. This means that it has the function of linking one thought to another, showing that the two ideas (sentences) are closely related. If we were simply to replace the semi-colon with a period, this concept of a close relationship is lost.

Bad: ABM had an excellent year, they are going to order new computers for everyone.

Bad: ABM had an excellent year. They are going to order new computers for everyone.

Good: ABM had an excellent year; they are going to order new computers for everyone.

Note that it is possible to use a comma if you use an introductory conjunction, as the pattern in #2 illustrates, above.

Good: Since ABM had an excellent year, they are going to order new computers for everyone.

No comma is necessary, of course, if you employ the simple coordinate sentence structure illustrated in #1, above.

Good: **ABM bought everyone new computers *after* their sales increased more than expected.**

But here too, we often find commas placed before the conjunction, especially when the two ideas that are linked are somewhat in opposition (using conjunctions such as *but*, *yet* and even *so*).

Good: **ABM had an excellent year, *so* they are going to order new computers for everyone.**

Examples.

Bad: The merger will be completed next week, everyone should wait until then before they decide whether to take the early-out option.

Good: **Since the merger will be completed next week, everyone should wait until then before they decide whether to take the early-out option.**

Bad: Last year it rained much more than usual, the rice crops were less than hoped for.

Good: **Last year it rained much more than usual, so the rice crops were less than hoped for.**
(or)
Good: **Since last year it rained much more than usual, the rice crops were less than hoped for.**

Bad: I answer phones, I type dictation.

Good: **I answer phones and I type dictation.**

Bad: They are the leaders in the area for home electronics, they sell more in a month than many stores sell in a year.

Good: **They are the leaders in the area for home electronics; they sell more in a month than many stores sell in a year.**

Bad: All new employees must pass the physical examination, the job is quite demanding.

Good: **Since the job is quite demanding, all new employees must pass the physical examination.**

III. PRINCIPLE OF ECONOMY – B. SENTENCE LEVEL.
c. DISCUSS ONE POINT PER STATEMENT

(65) <u>Avoid Unrelated Ideas in the Same Sentence.</u>

Here, we look at the kinds of distractions that arise from discussing more than one point per statement. If the points are unrelated, the overall point of the statement is likely to be confusing for the readers. In these situations, it is usually best to simply split the statements up into their independent thought units, and create separate sentences. Sometimes there are several statements seemingly related to each other, but if the number is too great, we will want to break the statements up into more manageable units.

A statement that contains two distinct ideas needs to be separated:

Bad: A staff meeting is scheduled for this Friday at 4 PM, also everyone should turn in their new pay vouchers to the personnel section.

Good: **A staff meeting is scheduled for this Friday at 4 PM. Also, everyone should turn in their new pay vouchers to the personnel section.**

When you have many items to discuss, it is best to arrange the items into groups, or categories, and treat each group individually in a single series of statements, rather than attempting to combine everything into one lengthy statement.

Bad: I am writing to you to let you know about the travel plans for the three supervisors. Mr. Robson will be visiting New York the first week of May, Boston during the second week, and San Francisco during the third week, Ms. Suzuki will go to San Francisco first, then she will go to New York, and finish up in Boston, while Mr. Itoh will spend the first two weeks in San Francisco, followed by a week in New York.

Good: **I am writing to you to let you know about the travel plans for the three supervisors. First, Mr. Robson will be visiting New York the first week of May, Boston during the second week, and San Francisco during the third week. Second, Ms. Suzuki will go to San Francisco first, then she will go to New York, and finish up in Boston. Finally, Mr. Itoh will spend the first two weeks in San Francisco, followed by a week in New York.**

In the last set of examples, we chose to organize the statements by *person* (Mr. Robson, Ms. Suzuki and Mr. Itoh), but in similar situations we may prefer to order things *chronologically* (where everyone is going to be first, where they are going to be second, etc.) or *spatially* (in this case, by city: Mr. Robson will be in New York during the first week of May, Ms. Suzuki will visit New York during the second week, and Mr. Itoh will visit there during the third week...), or by any number of other organizational criteria.

Examples.

Bad: We need to purchase an extra one hundred pounds of meat from Pacific Distributors this week, and contact Mr. Johnson to see if you can arrange a meeting for later this month.

Good: We need to purchase an extra one hundred pounds of meat from Pacific Distributors this week. Also, please contact Mr. Johnson to see if you can arrange a meeting for later this month.

- -

Bad: I would like to make arrangements for a two-bedroom suite for the week in June beginning on the twentieth, and do you have a business center there?

Good: I would like to make arrangements for a two-bedroom suite for the week in June beginning on the twentieth. Further, do you have a business center there?

- -

Bad: Please record all of your expenses in a travel log, and only purchase your train tickets from Yasui Travels.

Good: Please record all of your expenses in a travel log. Also, we ask that you only purchase your train tickets from Yasui Travels.

- -

Bad: Employees are free to help themselves to anything in the supply cabinet, but the restrooms on the first floor are for customers only.

Good: Employees are free to help themselves to anything in the supply cabinet. However, I would like to point out that the restrooms on the first floor are for customers only.

- -

III. PRINCIPLE OF ECONOMY – C. PARAGRAPH LEVEL.
a. BRIEF IS BEST: FEWER SENTENCES ARE PREFERRED TO EXPANDED DISCOURSE

(66)   Underwrite, rather than Overwrite.

Overwriting can come in many forms. Overwriting can mean the overuse of unnecessarily fancy terms, it can mean the overuse of adjectives and adverbs, and it can mean the restating of your ideas to the point of distraction or with too much enthusiasm.

First, we want to avoid overly informal conversational expressions on the one hand, but we also want to avoid the use of uncommon low frequency expressions on the other hand. It is distracting for the reader to have to deal with obscure terms that no one uses. Readers' reactions range from simple lack of understanding, to resentment, to distrust. No one wants to come across a word that they don't know, and few will have the time or energy to look up the term in a dictionary. The impression left with the reader, however, will usually be negative; the reader may think the writer is trying too hard to impress others with his knowledge, or, the reader will simply be annoyed at the lack of clarity.

When overwriting occurs at the paragraph level, it usually involves exaggeration on the one hand, or lack of confidence on the other. A writer may try to patch up, or protect, his ideas by filling every possible gap in his argument, where a good argument, elegantly written, should stand alone without a lot of extra padding. Often, poor writers restate the main point they are trying to make in several different ways to ensure that the reader will get the message. While at first glance this seems like a good strategy, an even better strategy is simply to express the original thought in a clear and precise manner to begin with, so that restatement is not necessary.

Overwriting also comes out of a certain blindness that the writer has with his topic. Usually the writer *knows* well what he wants to say, and upon rereading his text, is sure that he has said what he intended, even though in reality there may be some points that can be easily misunderstood by the reader. The reader may not share the writer's excitement about the subject, and when the writer's excitement overflows onto the pages of his text, this can often be very distracting to the reader. So, in this sense, overwriting can result from the writer losing sight of the need to be neutral in expressing his arguments, and getting caught up in the blind enthusiasm that may not be shared by his readers.

Finally, overwriting can simply result from the writer telling us too much. This may include the listing of unnecessary facts, details, information, opinions and the like. In professional writing, it is best to get to the main point directly and economically, not burdening the reader with unnecessary diversions, irrelevant information and pointless discussions.

Examples.

Bad: The important thing to remember is that metal chopsticks are environmentally friendly. They can be washed and reused hundreds of times. They do not contribute to a depletion of our forests. Using metal chopsticks can help protect our environment.

Good: **The important thing to remember is that metal chopsticks are environmentally friendly. They can be washed and reused hundreds of times, and since they are not made of wood they do not contribute to a depletion of our forests.**

Bad: The arguments against the proposal are weak when compared to those supporting it. One argument against is simply ridiculous, how could anyone assume that we could save money by collecting water in the winter from unused swimming pools? Whoever proposed such an idea obviously didn't think the idea through carefully. However, the arguments supporting the proposal [...].

Good: **The arguments against the proposal are weak when compared to those supporting it. However, the arguments supporting the proposal [...].**

Bad: To conclude, natural gas stoves are better in nearly every way over kerosene stoves. Natural gas stoves burn cleaner, natural gas stoves are safer, and natural gas stoves are nearly identical in cost to kerosene stoves.

Good: To conclude, natural gas stoves are better in nearly every way over kerosene stoves. Natural gas stoves burn cleaner, are safer, and are nearly identical in cost to kerosene stoves.

Bad: I think we should buy from Tanaka, Inc. My sister knows the owner personally, and she says that they are very honest people. Their products have an excellent reputation.

Good: I think we should buy from Tanaka, Inc. Their products have an excellent reputation.

III. PRINCIPLE OF ECONOMY – C. PARAGRAPH LEVEL.
a. BRIEF IS BEST: FEWER SENTENCES ARE PREFERRED TO EXPANDED DISCOURSE

(67)   Be Brief and Concise: Break Writing into Short Sections.

Certainly the essence of economy in writing is to be brief and to the point. Write as if your audience's time is valuable, and do not burden them with anything that is unnecessary. One way to do this is to imagine that you are the person responsible for briefing the Prime Minister every morning on all important issues that he needs to know about before he goes about his daily activities. The Prime Minister likely does not have much time for this briefing session, so it is necessary to choose only those issues that are of the highest importance, and then, determine what exactly constitutes the key information. These messages must be compact, precise, accurate and clear. They must not contain any irrelevant information, or any distractions. Your success is measured by your ability to cover as much information as necessary in as brief an amount of time as possible.

Although most of us will never find ourselves in such a demanding position as described above, the points made are just as relevant to the people we do interact with professionally, and their time should be considered no less valuable. The *"brief is best"* axiom is particularly important for memos and letters, especially ones that require the reader to take action. The text should address only those points that are necessary, and should clearly spell out who should take an action, what kind of action to take, and how to take it.

When our text must necessarily contain a great deal of information, it is best to break an overly long sentence up into smaller units, even if the larger sentence is structurally correct and contains clauses all relating to a single idea. Similarly, at the paragraph level, when we have a paragraph that is overly long, it becomes cumbersome, dense, and often unfathomable. To prevent disinterest or distraction, it is best to break these overly long paragraphs up into more manageable shorter sections, or at least make slight transitions from one point to the next. This can be done by simply making paragraph breaks at transition points, where words such as *therefore, also, meanwhile, accordingly, nevertheless, thus,* and so forth are usually employed to signal a transition, or movement, in the discussion or any of the basic coordinate conjunctions (*also, but, still,* etc.).

> Examples.

Bad: Next week we will be having a meeting to discuss the problems associated with the possible lay-offs here at the Philadelphia plant. I am interested in looking into ideas that will allow us to retain as many long time employees as possible, but we don't need to worry too much about the summer temporary employment program. Also, we don't need to be concerned about the recently hired part-timers, we will worry about them at another time.

Good: **Next week we will have a meeting to discuss the possible lay-offs here at the Philadelphia plant. Specifically, I am interested in hearing ideas that will allow us to retain as many long time employees as possible. You need not worry about the temporary or part time employees at this time.**

Bad: Several people are expected to visit the plant next week, including members of the employee's trade union, an auditing team from headquarters and a design group that will be here to review our five-year growth plan. The only people you need to meet, however, are the auditors. You are expected to meet with them at 8 AM Wednesday morning in your office.

Good: **Several people will be visiting the plant next week, but the only people you need to meet are an auditing team from headquarters. You are expected to meet with them at 8 AM Wednesday morning in your office.**

Bad: There are three kinds of orders that we make. One is where we pay with cash transfer from our bank. The second type of order is a cash only order. This is done for small office supplies. The third kind is COD, but we actually never order this way.

Good: **There are two kinds of orders that we make. One is where we pay with cash transfer from our bank. The other type of order is a cash only order. This is done for small office supplies.**

III. PRINCIPLE OF ECONOMY – C. PARAGRAPH LEVEL.
b. DISCUSS ONE POINT PER STATEMENT

(68) <u>Develop Your Discussion One Step at a Time by Working from the Known to the Unknown.</u>

The first half of this rule comes naturally if you simply follow the basic principle of *discussing one point per statement*. By discussing one point per statement, the argument can of course proceed no faster than *one step at a time*. However, it is important to point out here that one step at a time also implies that the argument should move forward without *skipping* any intermediate steps. As for the second half of the rule, *working from the known to the unknown*, the implication here is not to start the discussion at a point that is unfamiliar to the reader. We will deal with this second point below.

When we are writing about something that contains information, ideas, and positions that the audience may not have seen before, it is important to start out on familiar grounds, then gradually work towards the new information, working from *outline to detail*, or working from *general to specific*. In each case, we want to begin with a review of the key elements of the discussion, and establish a familiar foundation upon which we are going to build our discussion. This review will give readers a chance to be reminded of facts that they may have been exposed to before, but have since forgotten, or failed to see their relevance to the current discussion. By reviewing the basic elements, everyone is familiar with at least the ideas upon which your observations are based. Then, one step at a time, take the reader from this firm foundation through the relevant points that lead directly to your new points.

Determining a proper starting point (exactly how far back you have to go, or how basic you have to be), depends, of course, entirely upon having an accurate understanding of your audience. In situations where it is not totally clear how much your audience knows, it is always best to *underestimate* your audience slightly, rather than overestimate their abilities to handle the new concepts. At first this might seem to be a contradiction of some of the advice given in other rules, where we are encouraged to write to the appropriate level of our audience, rather than beneath it, so that we don't appear to be talking down to our readers. However, the point made here differs slightly. When we talk about writing to the appropriate level of our audience, we are talking about *"levels of formality," "levels of overall technical expertise,"* and so forth. Here, when we talk about starting our discussion at a point slightly beneath the expected threshold of our audience, we are simply talking about the <u>point in a sequential argument</u>, an argument made up of facts. It is better to start a sequence at a stage (with a basic set of facts) that the audience is familiar with, and move from the familiar point to the unfamiliar, rather than to start at a point well into the sequence, where some readers may never be able to catch up, or fill in the key missing elements from the earlier stages of the argument.

> Examples.

Bad: The mora has recently been used to describe a constituent of the syllable, with a metrical structure of its own. The mora can also be used to describe metrical elements of many languages.

Good: **The basic sound unit in linguistics is usually the syllable. This unit is used to describe the basic metrical structure found in most languages. The mora, on the other hand, has recently been used to describe a constituent of the syllable, with a metrical structure of its own. The mora can also be used to describe the metrical elements of many languages.**

- -

Bad: Most colleges have some sort of computer assisted language instruction systems in their language labs.

Good: **For the last ten years or so, computers have been used to assist various forms of language training programs. Recently, most colleges have installed some sort of computer assisted language instruction (CALI) or computer assisted language learning (CALL) systems in their language labs.**

- -

Bad: In order to get on the World Wide Web (WWW), just log on to the Internet and access WWW. In getting on to the WWW, you will need special navigational software.

Good: **One of the exciting new developments in computer communications is the almost immediate access to information that is produced virtually anywhere in the world. The most common network that allows such instant access is the World Wide Web (WWW), on the Internet. In order to get on WWW, just log on to the Internet and access WWW. To access the WWW, you will need special navigational software, such as Firefox® or Explorer®.**

- -

IV. PRINCIPLE OF APPROPRIATENESS

Overview

The ***Principle of Appropriateness*** consists of four supporting rules: 1) Be truthful and show politeness and respect for others; 2) Avoid idioms and slang, especially the more obscure regional variations; 3) Avoid contractions and casual speech rules, and; 4) Use grammatically correct sentences. This principle basically guides proper usage of the English language. It gives guidelines for avoiding offensive and counterproductive writing styles, and helps to ensure an accurate use of the basic rules of English. This principle can screen out language that is unsuitable for written text; language that may otherwise be perfectly fine when spoken.

The first rule, ***Be truthful and show politeness and respect for others***, suggests that it is always best to use a certain degree of care and control when you put your thoughts down on paper, even when you are upset, or when you strongly disagree with something or someone. In general, as mentioned earlier, it is best to adopt a familiar comfortable writing style that is respectful of others and is at least moderately polite. Of course your audience will determine just how formal, or how polite you should be, but for our purposes here, it is important to simply note that we should always avoid making generalizations, stereotypes and other comments that serve to demean someone or some group. Similarly, some words are culturally loaded, and should be avoided on paper. We look at how to handle gender roles in writing, and provide reasonable choices that serve to reduce the chances of others taking offense at your writing. Also, in terms of being truthful, on the surface it means to simply represent things as they are, not what you would like them to be. We want to avoid misleading the audience, or implying that things are different than they really are. Further, though, it is important to state clearly if you agree with something, accept something, like something, and so forth, since once you have committed your comment to paper, you are on record for those opinions. This can become problematic when you show a tolerance for something that you really are not interested in, since you may find yourself in a position later where you will have to retract your earlier (false) statement.

The second rule, ***Avoid idioms and slang, especially the more obscure***

regional variations, is particularly important for writing, since nothing looks more out of place in a business letter than poorly understood idioms, or inappropriate slang. While some speakers can get away with using regional slang and colloquialisms, the written text format is not appropriate for such expression. We look at some basic guidelines regarding what kinds of expressions are best to avoid.

The third rule, ***Avoid contractions and casual speech rules***, is similar to rule two, where both suggest that it is best not to use speech forms that are suitable for casual conversation in business writing. While some contractions are not only acceptable, but useful, in written text, some of the more obscure variations are clearly unsuitable. Similarly, phrases and short cuts that are regularly used in casual conversation are rarely useful in a written context, and when employed, serve to detract from the overall message of the text.

The fourth rule, ***Use grammatically correct sentences***, may seem obvious and not even worthy of mention. Here, we focus on four of the areas that cause the greatest amount of difficulty in writing good English. I point out the causes for the majority of errors in these four areas, and offer some basic guidelines for dealing with these mistakes. Specifically, we look at linking subject number to the proper verb forms, understanding key differences between certain prepositions, how to avoid words that are left stranded at the ends of sentences and how to avoid incomplete sentences.

IV. PRINCIPLE OF APPROPRIATENESS – A. WORD LEVEL.
a. BE TRUTHFUL AND SHOW POLITENESS AND RESPECT FOR OTHERS

(69)   Use Appropriate Gender References.

Back in the 1970's, there was a movement to attempt to overcome the sexism that exists in the English language. Some authors replaced *him* with *her*, *he* with *she*, *chairman* with *chairwoman*, and so forth. Others attempted complete neutralization by employing *one* (instead of *he* or *she*), *chairperson* (instead of *chairman* or *chairwoman*), and so forth. In this discussion I will try to provide an acceptable range for the writer to choose from, hopefully providing something suitable for his (or her) own style.

First of all, some terms to avoid: Avoid using slashed words such as *s/he* or *he/she*. Use of slashed words quickly becomes problematic when issues of subject agreement come up, such as when possessive or reflexive pronouns are required. In this case, *one* is a better neutral substitute (or, even better, the more personal *you*). In most texts, however, the third person singular male pronouns are still the most common (*he, his* and *him*), and represent approximately 75% of the forms found in professional texts, written by males or females. In professional writing, then, you are not wrong to use these "male" forms, and for most people the forms are really quite neutral. If you do feel it necessary to find a *completely neutral approach*, change your reference to *third person plural (they, their, theirs)*.

A new employee must check in with his supervisor at 8 AM each day. ("sexist")
Employees must check in with their supervisor at 8 AM each day. (neutral)
You must check in with your supervisor at 8 AM each day. (neutral & personal)

There are a lot of nouns that carry with them some marking for gender, such as *steward* and *stewardess, actor* and *actress, bride* (forget *bridegroom*) and *groom*, etc. For these few word pairs, there is of course no confusion. But, what about *men* who are *nurses, woman* who are *chairmen*, and so forth? We can have a *male nurse*, but we can't have a **woman chairman* (though some have suggested *madam chairman*, or simply, *chairwoman*). Often it is simply easier to remove the gender reference entirely, and use *nurse* and *chair* as neutral titles. Is there an easy way out of this? Unfortunately, there isn't, but most situations do not require you to make such a decision, just follow the standards appropriate for your field, and when in doubt about a person's title, ask the person directly, or someone who likely has the information.

Finally, there are a few interesting areas where gender does follow some prescribed guidelines. For example, when we refer to *inanimate objects* such as ships, countries, tractors, etc., we refer to them by the third person singular feminine pronouns *(she, her, hers)*. However, *animate creatures* including insects and animals (such as spiders or monkeys), where the sex is difficult to determine, are referred to by the *masculine pronouns (he, him, his)*.

Examples.

Bad: The manager requires that each employee undergoes a thorough background check before he will give an employee permanent status.
Good: **The manager requires that all employees undergo a thorough background check before an employee will be given permanent status.**

- -

Bad: He (or she) should have made reservations by him/herself, and not rely on the secretary for such purposes.
Good: **Employees should make reservations by themselves, and not rely on the secretary for such purposes.**

- -

Bad: Whether he is trying to translate Mandarin into English or he is simply writing original text in English, he must be able to articulate the important cultural differences.
Better: **Whether one is trying to translate Mandarin into English or one is simply writing original text in English, one must be able to articulate the important cultural differences.**
Best: **Whether you are trying to translate Mandarin into English or you are simply writing original text in English, you must be able to articulate the important cultural differences.**
(or)
Best: **Whether trying to translate Mandarin into English or simply writing original text in English, important cultural differences must be clearly articulated.**

- -

IV. PRINCIPLE OF APPROPRIATENESS – A. WORD LEVEL.
a. BE TRUTHFUL AND SHOW POLITENESS AND RESPECT FOR OTHERS

(70) <u>Use Neutral Words.</u>

It is essential to avoid culturally loaded terms in business writing. These terms usually refer to people, race, religions and creeds, but are rarely the terms used by the people themselves for whom the terms are being applied. Usually any nickname that refers to the group a person is a member of is not appropriate.

A common group of culturally loaded words to avoid are words that refer to a person's country of origin. Nicknames such as *yanks* for Americans, *limies* for the Irish, *japs* for the Japanese, *aussies* for Australians and *krauts* for Germans are among the list of <u>loaded words</u> that <u>should be avoided at all costs.</u> Virtually any other <u>nickname</u> for a <u>national group is</u> equally <u>inappropriate</u>.

Individual cultural and/or ethnic groups that exist within a multi-cultural society such as the U.S. are slightly more difficult to come to grips with. In the U.S., most ethnic groups these days have come to accept the "hyphenated-American" approach. These terms include *Japanese-Americans, Chinese-Americans, Black-Americans*, and so forth. Some have suggested that while terms such as Japanese-Americans and Chinese-Americans indicate the cultural identity of the group, the term Black-American merely indicates the color of a person's skin, with no direct relation to a particular culture. For this reason, the term Afro-American was once in favor, but has recently been replaced with *African-American*.

These arguments apply equally to religions as well. We rarely refer to followers of the *Jewish* faith as *Jews*, or to *White Anglo Saxon Protestants* as *WASPS*, and so forth. Similarly, it is not appropriate to refer to the gay population with terms such as *queens, dikes, fairies*, and so forth. Finally, it is not appropriate to single out one particular group of any society and make claims that suggest that these groups are either in some way inferior, or superior, to others. For this reason, words such as *blind, deaf, crippled*, and so forth have fallen out of favor, replaced by *visually impaired, hearing impaired, wheelchair-bound* and other more neutral terms.

Some terms continue to change as ideas, beliefs, attitudes and values change, so what is appropriate today may not be appropriate tomorrow. For the most part, however, few of us will ever need to deal with these questions, since it is almost never necessary to refer to any one particular cultural or ethnic group exclusively in business and technical writing. Simply the fact of selecting one group out for any reason is contrary to good writing and usually quite unprofessional. Frequently we can neutralize our statements by substituting *many*, or *many people*, instead of the culturally loaded expressions. Usually this substitution still allows us to convey the same basic points, but in a much less offensive manner.

Examples.

Bad: Since farmers are usually just country bumpkins, they can't be expected to understand all of the complexities of the modern day hi-tech agribusiness.
Good: **Many long-time farmers do not understand all of the complexities of the modern day hi-tech agribusiness.**

Bad: The part-time female teachers are just a bunch of housewives.
Good: **The part-time teachers are skilled professionals.**

Bad: We all know that they are workaholics and that they never spend a dime.
Good: **Many are hard working and thrifty.**

Bad: Soda-jerks don't need job security, they just need a paycheck.
Good: **Part-time ice cream store workers don't need job security, they just need a paycheck.**

Bad: Since you're crippled, we will be happy to provide an office for you on the first floor, so that you don't have to worry about getting up the stairs.
Good: **We are assigning you to an office on the first floor, which is fully wheel-chair accessible.**

Bad: Many novice employees are ignorant about plant operations.
Good: **Many novice employees are unaware of all of the plant's operations.**

IV. PRINCIPLE OF APPROPRIATENESS – A. WORD LEVEL.
b. AVOID IDIOMS AND SLANG, ESPECIALLY THE MORE OBSCURE REGIONAL VARIATIONS

(71)   Avoid Colloquialisms, Clichés, Slang and Regional Expressions.

In general it is best to use neutral words in all situations, and not resort to culturally loaded words (as the last rule suggested). Here, we discourage the use of terms that are more commonly used in casual conversation than in business writing. These forms include slang, colloquialisms, clichés and regional expressions.

It is especially important to avoid *slang*, since slang expressions basically are expressions that differ from the normal language by breaking syntactic or lexical rules. In other words, slang, by definition, are language forms that do not follow the standard rules of English. Language forms that break the basic rules of English have no place in professional writing. Slang expressions such as "stop *dissing* him" (from "stop disrespecting him") are not appropriate in professional applications.

Similarly, *colloquialisms* are not suitable for most writing. These are basically informal speech forms that are more frequently heard in casual conversations among friends. Italicized expressions in the following examples are all out of place: "get to the *bare bones* of the problem," "this is really something that I think we can all *sink our teeth into*," and "*don't bite the hand that feeds you.*" While many of you may have spent a good deal of time learning various idiomatic expressions in English, it is best to avoid these idioms, especially if they are particularly colorful and abstract, such as the examples illustrated above.

Regional expressions are to be avoided for the simple reason that others outside of the region in which the expressions are based may read your text at some point and may mistake these terms for something completely different. It is sometimes hard to determine if an expression is regional or not, so when in doubt, leave it out. Generally the reasons for avoiding colloquial expressions, cited above, apply equally here. "Regional" may sometimes not be a specific physical region (such as Northern America), but it may be corporate, or industry-specific (such as terms adopted by a large computer firm for their in-house correspondences). Of particular concern here is the use of food terms, where, depending upon the region, a drink such as a *milk shake* may be referred to as a *malted* in one area, a *shake* in another and a *mixer* in another.

Finally, clichés are to be avoided as well, since they usually serve to render your text too casual for the work place. Clichés are simply overused expressions that may be permissible idioms (they are straightforward, not colorful or abstract) but they are simply too formulaic and unimaginative. Examples of these expressions include *"bottom line," "dos and don'ts," "run it by," "nonplussed," "up to speed"* and so forth.

| Examples. |

Bad: Well, greetings and salutations! I hope you all are enjoying the spring as much as I have been.
Good: Greetings everyone. I hope you are enjoying the spring as much as I am.

Bad: We'd like to concentrate our sales in "The City," and later, extend to the rest of the "Bay Area."
Good: We'd like to concentrate our sales in San Francisco and later extend to the rest of Marin County.

Bad: The long and the short of it is we no longer have any funds available for investments.
Good: In short, we no longer have any funds available for investments.

Bad: I am pleased to report that the review of the plant operations determined that everything was copacetic.
Good: I am pleased to report that the review of the plant operations determined that everything was excellent.

Bad: The average English-speaking Taiwanese is nonplussed when I ask them which language they are referring to when they say Taiwanese.
Good: The average English-speaking Taiwanese is confused when I ask them which language they are referring to when they say "Taiwanese."

Bad: The ends of the company are served by finalizing the sales agreement.
Good: Finalizing the sales agreement would be beneficial to the company.

IV. PRINCIPLE OF APPROPRIATENESS – A. WORD LEVEL.
c. AVOID CONTRACTIONS AND CASUAL SPEECH RULES

(72)   Avoid Uncommon Contractions.

Contractions are words that are usually formed from the combination of two words: A *verb* and the negative *not*, or; a *pronoun* and a form of the *be* verb (or an auxiliary verb such as *will, would* and *have*). Examples of the first type are *aren't, haven't, won't* etc., while examples of the second type include *it's, she's, they're, we'd, he'll*, etc. Avoid making contractions with personal names, or other regular nouns (e.g.. **Susan'll, *manager'd*).

Using contractions such as *don't, can't, it's* and *they're* is allowed in business writing, but it must be understood that contractions do convey a sense of informality, so overuse of contractions tend to render your writing overly familiar. In some applications, such as informal memos to the staff, this is acceptable, but the more formal the writing is, the fewer the contractions there should be. So, expressions like the following are perfectly acceptable: "*so please don't hesitate to call me if you have any questions,*" and; "*shouldn't we just throw out the old plan and start all over again?*" On the other hand, when a document requires formality, it is best to avoid contractions, thereby ensuring a greater degree of authority and distance: "*I will not allow anyone to smoke in the company automobiles*" or; "*I am sorry but we could not grant your request.*"

There are times when a situation seems to require an unusual contraction, or an uncommon one. Usually it is best simply not to contract the two forms in these situations, since the contracted forms often look odd, disjointed and out of place. For example, replace *mustn't* with *must not, needn't* with *need not, shan't* with *shall not, mightn't* with *might not, mayn't* with *may not*, and *ain't* with *am not*. (or *are not*). In no cases should the writer create new contractions (such as creating **havingn't* from *having not*--from *not having*).

It is also important to distinguish between contractions and possessives. For example, *Bob's car* is fine (indicating possession), but not **Bob's going* (it is better to simply state, *Bob is going*). Similarly, *the company's insurance* (again, indicating possession) is fine, but not **the company's going to merge* (it is better to state: *the company is going to merge*).

> Examples.

Bad: We mustn't allow any shipments to be sent during the last week of the month.

Good: We must not allow any shipments to be sent during the last week of the month.

Bad: The manager's attending the conference in Boston all this week, so Taeko's the acting supervisor.

Good: The manager is attending the conference in Boston all this week, so Taeko is the acting supervisor.

Bad: We'll be considerin' you're proposals as soon as it's possible.

Good: We'll consider your proposals as soon as we can.

Bad: The boss'll meet all new employees on their first day of work. Before the meeting, you'll need to fill out some personnel forms.

Good: The boss will meet all new employees on their first day of work. Before the meeting, you'll need to fill out some personnel forms.

Bad: What's it to them if I don't pay my bill on time?

Good: Why are they so concerned about whether I pay my bill on time?

Bad: Why'd you go and hafta spoil the plan?

Good: It was not necessary to spoil the plan.

IV. PRINCIPLE OF APPROPRIATENESS – B. SENTENCE LEVEL.
a. BE TRUTHFUL AND SHOW POLITENESS AND RESPECT FOR OTHERS

(73)   <u>Tell the Truth.</u>

Whenever you write something for the purpose of sharing information with someone else, you are creating a permanent record of your thoughts. Because of this permanency, there is a tendency to treat the written word as more binding than the spoken word. In U.S. courts, for example, written proofs of contract are much more powerful than agreements made only by spoken promises. So, in the extreme case, written (and signed) documents which contain promises and agreements can often be used to hold someone accountable.

It is useful, therefore, to remember that written notes have the tendency to <u>establish</u> definite opinion, obligation or expectation. So, for example, if you have been asked to write a recommendation for a former colleague (a person you really didn't think is qualified), you should take care not to say things that are not true about the individual. Often, in writing recommendations, there is a tendency to exaggerate, or inflate, the real abilities and potential of the person being recommended. However, if the person really is not qualified, but is hired on the basis of your recommendation, then it is you, ultimately, who will suffer some measure of discredit, where your opinion will no longer be treated as highly.

Similarly, for another example, if you are asked to attend a trade show on behalf of someone else, and you actually hate going to trade shows, it is not appropriate to make up some excuse for not being able to attend. If you wrote that you are pleased to be asked to attend, but due to a prior engagement, you are unable to do so, then you are simply opening the door for another invitation later, which (since you don't like trade shows) will require another refusal for one reason or another. It is best simply to decline the first invitation, by saying that you would prefer not to attend events such as trade shows, and that someone else might benefit from the experience (and suggest an alternate). In this way you are truthfully replying that you are not interested in attending, though you appreciate the consideration, and at the same time you have offered a constructive suggestion that may be used to remedy the situation. Finally, if you have no excuse to refuse a proposal, don't make one up, just decline gracefully--you don't need to make something up.

> Examples.

Bad: I really would like to go bowling with your company team this Friday evening, but unfortunately, I have a meeting I must attend.

Good: **I am sorry that I can't join your team this Friday; I am afraid that I never really learned to enjoy the game.**

Bad: Ms. Beckman is quite simply the best employee I have had the pleasure of working with. There is nothing she can't do.

Good: **Ms. Beckman is one of the best employees I have had the pleasure of working with. She is very capable and can handle most work tasks efficiently and professionally.**

Bad: I would be very happy to accept your offer of speaking to the No Hope for Reform Society at Toledo Prison.

Good: **I regret that I would prefer not to address the No Hope for Reform Society, so I respectfully decline your offer.**

Bad: The samples that you sent us were of very fine quality. Although we are unable to make a purchase at this time, we will likely order from you in the near future.

Good: **We were not impressed by the quality of the samples that you recently sent us. We ask that you remove us from your mailing list.**

Bad: If you do not vacate the building by 5 PM September 1, I, and some of my larger assistants, will personally assist in throwing you out.

Good: **You are requested to vacate the building by 5 PM September 1. If you fail to honor this request, I will turn the problem over to the police.**

IV. PRINCIPLE OF APPROPRIATENESS – B. SENTENCE LEVEL.
a. BE TRUTHFUL AND SHOW POLITENESS AND RESPECT FOR OTHERS

(74)   Avoid Sweeping Generalizations and Stereotyping.

Sometimes, in order to be persuasive, we are tempted to let individual facts appear as if they are part of a larger set of similar facts, allowing a single point to appear as if it stood for much broader implications. Other times, we know only a few relevant facts, yet we are tempted to make statements and generalizations based on these facts, as if they were all that were necessary. In many ways, making sweeping generalizations is similar to overstatement and exaggeration, however, the difference lies in the fact that generalizations are used to cover up what we don't know, while exaggeration simply expands upon the facts, making them look broader, stronger and more relevant than they really are.

Generalizations, then, require the reader to accept the points that you have made to stand for something larger than they really do. In other words, if you have learned that some people would prefer light mayonnaise as opposed to high cholesterol mayonnaise in your chicken burgers, a generalization would be that all people preferred such a choice. *Exaggeration* suggests that things are *more* than they really are, and thus, are a *distortion* of the facts. A *Generalization*, on the other hand, *allows the few facts to represent the rule*, usually as if it were one hundred percent correct. In a sense, then, a generalization is treated as *an absolute*. Many times, of course, generalizations are not based on facts at all, instead, they simply are what the writer believes, or in some cases, simply what he values. So, if six out of ten people said that they preferred light mayonnaise to regular, an exaggeration would be something like "*a significant majority of people favor light mayonnaise over regular mayonnaise,*" while a generalization would be "*people prefer light mayonnaise over regular mayonnaise.*"

Since generalizations are not well-founded in fact, they should usually be avoided when writing in a professional context. They are, in many ways, simply opinions that we have dressed up to look like facts.

> Examples.

Bad: Everyone likes coffee, so, we are starting a new policy where all employees must contribute $10 per month to the coffee fund.

Good: **If you are a coffee drinker, you are asked to contribute $10 per month to the coffee fund.**

- -

Bad: People who live in the Southwest all love hot spicy foods.

Good: **Many people who live in the Southwest enjoy hot spicy foods.**
(or)
Good: **Our research has determined that many people who live in the Southwest enjoy hot spicy foods.**
(or)
Good: **Recent surveys indicate that many people who live in the Southwest enjoy hot spicy foods.**

- -

Bad: The board of directors are really not interested in the day to day administration of the company.

Good: **Several members of the board of directors have stated that they are not interested in the day to day administration of the company.**

- -

Bad: Children who watch too much violence on TV will gradually confuse the difference between reality and fantasy, and will themselves become violent and aggressive.

Good: **No legitimate research study has ever demonstrated that children who watch too much violence on TV will gradually confuse the difference between reality and fantasy, and will themselves become violent and aggressive.**

- -

IV. PRINCIPLE OF APPROPRIATENESS – B. SENTENCE LEVEL.
a. BE TRUTHFUL AND SHOW POLITENESS AND RESPECT FOR OTHERS

(75)   Avoid Sexist, Racist and Prejudiced Comments.

When generalizations are made about a particular group of people, they are based upon observations that are usually very superficial and often quite negative. The result is a stereotyping of a group of people according to often unfavorable characteristics. Stereotypes are often based on sex, on race, on ethnicity and on other criteria that are used to define classes of people. (See Rule #70, above, for a related discussion on the use of neutral terms.)

People can be grouped according to any number of characteristics. They can be grouped according to *occupation* (engineers, doctors, teachers, etc.), they can be grouped according to *sex* (men, women), *age* (old/young, children/adults), *location* (people from a particular city (or state, or country)), *skill level* (beginner, intermediate, advanced) and so forth. Even the most harmless stereotype, such as "all engineers like to work with figures" cannot and does not apply to every member of the group to which it is referring. The problem with stereotypes, of course, is that *there are always exceptions to the rule,* and more than likely, the person who represents the exception will not react favorably to the generalization.

When you are speaking about a group, of which you are a member, it is sometimes permissible to refer to your particular group with some sort of sweeping generalization, though here too, you are likely to encounter a few (in your group) who do not share your point of view. Much more problematic, of course, is when you attempt to make generalizations about other groups, of which you are not a member. Reception to such generalizations will likely be cold at a minimum, and confrontational at the extreme. Some particularly delicate areas that you should never make sweeping generalizations on are *gender, race, religion, ethnicity, country of origin, families, personal convictions* and *personal values.* These generalizations include the association of common straits such as *strength* to any one class of people, or *intelligence,* or *diligence,* and any of a hundred other such behavioral characteristics: All such associations are to be avoided at all costs.

> Examples.

Bad: The older an employee is, the less productive the employee is.
Good: **There is no direct relationship between age and productivity.**

Bad: Men don't work as hard as women.
Good: **There is no direct relationship between gender and dedication to work.**

Bad: Just thank God that you still have a job.
Good: **Be thankful that you still have a job.**

Bad: Housewives aren't able to handle heavy jobs such as lifting heavy boxes, operating heavy machinery, etc.
Good: **Many workers aren't able to handle heavy jobs such as lifting heavy boxes, operating heavy machinery, etc.**

Bad: Men can't understand the amount of energy needed to raise children and keep house at the same time.
Good: **Many people can't understand the amount of energy needed to raise children and keep house at the same time.**

Bad: Many blacks today have achieved, though hard work and great personal sacrifice, greater success than their forebears ever thought possible.
Good: **Many people today have achieved, though hard work and great personal sacrifice, greater success than their forebears ever thought possible.**

Bad: Disabled people can't care for themselves.
Good: **Some people are unable to care for themselves.**

IV. PRINCIPLE OF APPROPRIATENESS – B. SENTENCE LEVEL.
b. USE GRAMMATICALLY CORRECT SENTENCES

(76)   Keep Tense and Number in Agreement.

Keeping tense and number in agreement is one of the basic rules of English that is frequently broken by non-native speakers. Problems with number and tense agreement can arise from several different sources. One source is when there are phrases placed between the subject and the verb which must agree with the subject. Another source is when the subject is a mass noun, and it is mistaken for a plural subject (mass nouns are of course always singular -- refer to Rule #9 for further discussion). Still another source is confusion over what constitutes the subject, and whether the subject is indeed plural or not. We will look at each of these problems separately below.

Sometimes the confusion about number references in a sentence is brought about by other phrases in the sentence that tend to mask, or hide, the connection between the subject and its reference. In these situations, it is advisable to simply look past these phrases, and make sure the subjects agree.

Bad: Your account, according to our records, are overdrawn.
Good: Your account, according to our records, is overdrawn.
(or, even better)
Good: According to our records, your account is overdrawn.

Other times, the confusion is a result of using mass nouns as subjects, where the adjectives seem to indicate a plural subject, but where in fact the subject is singular. The more confusing adjectives include *some, a lot* and *few*.

Bad: A lot of sugar are needed by the refinery.
Good: A lot of sugar is needed by the refinery.
(or)
Good: A large number of bags of sugar are needed by the refinery.

Along these same lines, *much* is often the source of confusion, where the most common error is mistaking it for meaning the equivalent of *a lot*. Rather, *much* is mainly used in questions ("how much?"), negative expressions ("not much") *so-that* and *too* expressions ("so much that"), and for mass nouns.

Good: How much money do you have?
Bad: I have much money.
Good: I don't have much money.
(or)
I have a lot of money.
(or)
I have so much money that I'll never be able to spend it all.

Sometimes the subject looks plural when in fact it is singular. This frequently happens when the subject is a business name such as *ABM Enterprises*, and *Star Systems*. Both of these company names, however, each refer to a single company, and therefore, to a single subject.

Bad: ABM Enterprises are going to order several new main frame computers.
Good: **ABM Enterprises is going to order several new main frame computers.**

Examples.

Bad: They have much money invested in raw materials.

Good: **They have a lot of money invested in raw materials.**

Bad: This year there are not so many cheap rice available.

Good: **This year there isn't so much cheap rice available.**

Bad: The box was delivered, but your orders was not included.

Good: **The box was delivered, but your orders were not included.**

Bad: Star Systems are going to introduce a new line of products carrying the

Wally World logo.

Good: **Star Systems is going to introduce a new line of products carrying the Wally World logo.**

Bad: The time schedule, which you list your overtime hours on, are available in the personal office.

Good: **The time schedule, on which you list your overtime hours, is available in the personal office.**
(or)
Good: **The time schedules, on which you list your overtime hours, are available in the personal office.**

Bad: You will need to do a few homeworks in order to complete the supervisor's training course.

Good: **You will need to do a little homework in order to complete the supervisor's training course.**

IV. PRINCIPLE OF APPROPRIATENESS – B. SENTENCE LEVEL.
b. USE GRAMMATICALLY CORRECT SENTENCES

(77) Choosing Prepositions.

Here, we focus on the most common mistakes of preposition usage, and note some general guidelines that can be used to help choose the best preposition for a specific sentence. In general, it is best to simply learn <u>verbs with appropriate prepositions as phrasal verbs (multi-word phrases)</u>, and, when there are several choices of prepositions, make a point to learn each verb-preposition pairing as an independent phrase, rather than simply learning verbs as one independent set of words, and prepositions as another set of independent words.

From and *of*. *From* is used when you are <u>indicating direction</u> in a literal sense, like "he came straight *from* his office," or, "he arrived *from* Tokyo early this morning." *Of*, on the other hand, is used to refer to what someone <u>represents, or is affiliated with</u>, such as "This is Mr. Suzuki *of* Star Systems" (not *from* Star Systems).

Of, on and *about*. In general, *about* and *on* both mean <u>concerning</u>, and though there are slight differences between the two, there isn't much confusion if one is substituted for the other. "I read a book *on* Mayan culture" and "I read a book *about* Mayan culture" are pretty much the same statements in terms of information. Many verb-preposition units are highly idiomatic, however, so the prepositions must be learned with their respective verbs. For example, *speak about, know about, concerned about,* but *briefed on, lectured on, commented on,* and *aware of, mindful of.* "The articles are *about* Mr. Morita" (not *of*). "This is Mr. Suzuki *of* Star Systems Enterprises" (not *on, about*). "The manager spoke to me *about* your problem" (not *on, of*). "You need to be aware *of* the fact that they do not hire foreigners to permanent positions" (not *on, about*). "You will be briefed *on* the new security policy" (not *about, of*).

Until and *by*. Until is used when you want <u>to indicate how long something can proceed</u> (as long as), while *by* is used <u>to indicate the point at which something must be completed</u> (before). "You have *until* 5 PM to finish the report" (not *by*), "You must finish the report *by* 5 PM" (not *until*).

With and *by*. "Stores are crowded *with* customers," not *by* customers. "Conventions are attended *by* professionals," not *with* professionals. Similarly, "He is associated *with* ABM," not by. "The answers were provided *by* the speaker" (not *with*). Similarly, you cut wires *with* pliers, not *by* pliers, you build things *with* your hands, not *by* your hands, but you contact people *by* telephone, not *with* telephone.

| Examples. |

Bad: All employees must finish their work until 5 PM. There is no overtime compensation.

Good: **All employees must finish their work by 5 PM. There is no overtime compensation.**

Bad: I have heard of the speaker, but I really know little on him. Could you send me some information of him for our announcements?

Good: **I have heard of the speaker, but I really know little about him. Could you send me some information on him for our announcements?**

Bad: The gardens are filled by new evergreens planted with volunteers.

Good: **The gardens are filled with new evergreens planted by volunteers.**

Bad: I am writing to you to introduce our company. I am Bill Breer from Omaha Enterprises, originally of Wisconsin.

Good: **I am writing to you to introduce our company. I am Bill Breer of Omaha Enterprises, originally based in Wisconsin.**

Bad: Please answer the questions of the new environmental regulations.

Good: **Please answer the questions about the new environmental regulations.**

Bad: On opening day, the restaurant was crowded by customers.

Good: **On opening day, the restaurant was crowded with customers.**

IV. PRINCIPLE OF APPROPRIATENESS – B. SENTENCE LEVEL.
b. USE GRAMMATICALLY CORRECT SENTENCES

(78)   Avoid Dangling Modifiers.

Dangling modifiers are modifiers that are not placed correctly within a sentence. These include *dangling participles*, which can be present participles (usually *verb + ing*), and sometimes the infinitive form, (*to + verb*), that do not have an appropriate subject to modify. Another example of a dangling modifier is one that is mistakenly associated to one subject, and not to the intended subject (usually the mistake is a result of having too much distance between the modifier and the subject).

A dangling participle looks like the progressive form of a verb, and is used incorrectly when it refers to the wrong subject.

Bad: Starting to eat, the boat left.
Good: Starting to eat, we left on the boat.
         (or)
Good: While I was starting to eat, the boat left.

In the first sentence above, the subject is we, but since it is not used in the text, it left the participle dangling (without an indication of the real subject). Observe a similar example:

Bad: The documents were discovered while searching for the tax receipts.
Good: The documents were discovered while they were searching for the tax receipts.

In the two sentences below, the modifying structure, "to develop effective writing skills," has an inappropriate subject in the first example (*individual effort*), since it requires a subject that is *capable* of writing something, therefore, the second example correctly has a stated human subject.

Bad: To develop effective writing skills, individual effort is required.
Good: For you to develop effective writing skills, individual effort is required.

A modifier can appear dangling, or at least confusing, if it is unclear what it is actually modifying. The cause of the problem here is that the modifier is too far from the subject that it modifies.

Bad: As the newest member of the management team, I would like to welcome you to company headquarters.
Good: **I would like to welcome you, the newest member of the management team, to company headquarters.**

In the first of the two examples directly above, it appears that the person speaking ("I") may in fact be the newest member of the management team, when it is in fact "you." By moving the modifier, it is now clear which person is being modified.

Examples.

Bad: Hearing the complaint, the meeting ended.
Good: **After hearing the complaint, the chairman called the meeting to an end.**

Bad: Failing to sell the required minimum, I have been asked to speak to you about improving sales.
Good: **I have been asked to speak to you about improving your sales since you failed to sell the required minimum.**

Bad: Using the new test instrument, many problems were encountered.
Good: **Using the new test instrument, we encountered many problems with the old data.**

Bad: The errors were erased while updating the database.
Good: **The errors were erased by the secretary while he was updating the database.**

Bad: To improve yearly profits, everyone's cooperation is necessary.
Good: **In order for Star Systems to improve their yearly profits, everyone's cooperation is necessary.**

Bad: As the only person opposed to the ban on smoking, I ask that you consider the alternatives.
Good: **I ask that you, the only person opposed to the ban on smoking, consider the alternatives.**

IV. PRINCIPLE OF APPROPRIATENESS – B. SENTENCE LEVEL.
b. USE GRAMMATICALLY CORRECT SENTENCES

(79)   Avoid Incomplete Sentences.

This is one of the final rules at the sentence level in this text, so we will review the basic sentence structure, and make some final observations regarding what actually constitutes a well constructed, grammatically correct sentence. Going back to the basic sentence order of *subject-verb-object*, we have suggested that this simple structure should be used to create all of your sentences in professional writing, or at least serve as a starting point. We have suggested that the *active voice* is better than the passive, and that *few modifying words and phrases are preferred* over many.

Rules #76-79 review four of the key areas that are often problematic for non-native speakers and writers of English. These four areas can be thought of as *conditions* on the basic S-V-O structure, which, if violated, render the sentence ungrammatical and, of course, incorrect. In most of the earlier discussions the rules were simply *guidelines* which can be employed to determine the best (clear, direct, precise) structure for a particular situation. In the last four rules we have specific rules which <u>*must* be adhered to</u>. With this in mind, we refer to what has now hopefully become a simple idea, namely, that *in order for sentences to be well-formed, they must be grammatically complete.*

Incomplete, or "fragmented," sentences are simply sentences that either have no clear subject, or no clear verb. Sentences can be complete, however, if there are no clear objects (*objects*, as discussed earlier, *are optional* even in our basic sentence structure), so in fact in its purest form our minimally acceptable basic sentence structure is actually S-V (not S-V-O).

Since we have discussed elsewhere the problem of missing nouns, and subjects, here we look at a final problem concerning missing verbs. Sentences without verbs occur rarely at the independent clause/single sentence level, but do appear frequently in compound and complex sentences. Here, the mistake is in assuming the verb of one clause is sufficient to carry the second clause.

Bad: The research department's interesting discovery of a new plastic resin that is cheaper to produce than anything else on the market.

Good: The research department's interesting discovery of a new plastic resin that is cheaper to produce than anything else on the market is welcome news indeed.

> Examples.

Bad: Hard work, discipline and dedication all into an excellent achievement.

Good: **Hard work, discipline and dedication all combined into an excellent achievement.**

Bad: They all worked very hard on the project. Expecting to produce the winning design entry.

Good: **They all worked very hard on the project, expecting to produce the winning design entry.**
(or)
Good: **Since they all worked very hard on the project, they expected to produce the winning design entry.**

Bad: Heavy schedules, poor equipment and, in the end, bad luck.

Good: **The project failed because of heavy schedules, poor equipment and, in the end, bad luck.**

Bad: The supplies were ordered last week, arriving by the end of the month.

Good: **The supplies were ordered last week and should arrive by the end of the month.**

Bad: The new recruits able, eager and dedicated.

Good: **The new recruits are able, eager and dedicated.**

IV. PRINCIPLE OF APPROPRIATENESS – C. PARAGRAPH LEVEL.
a. BE TRUTHFUL AND SHOW POLITENESS AND RESPECT FOR OTHERS

(80)   Use Neutral Tone: Avoid Inference and Implication.

In the earlier discussions I have suggested that we should avoid spite and sarcasm (Rule 48), and remain neutral (Rule 70). Here, we conclude with a consideration of writing in an appropriately neutral *tone*. Specifically, <u>we want to avoid inference, accusation, unsubstantiated (and perhaps unwanted) criticism, unfounded bias and misleading or misrepresented statements</u>.

In general, simply let the facts speak for themselves. If you don't have facts to support your opinions, then it is likely that your opinions do not, and perhaps cannot, hold much weight. It is best to leave these observations out. Alternatively, we are sometimes forced to discuss issues that we personally do not support. For example, perhaps you have been requested to contact all of the employees at your work place to see if you can enlist their support for an upcoming charity bazaar. You have been asked to send out a memo to all employees encouraging cooperation and support, but personally, you detest bazaars of any form, and it is the last thing that you would like to be involved with. If you let this personal view color the tone of your memo, your mission certainly will not be a successful one, and you will likely fail in the eyes of your supervisors. <u>A true professional can handle virtually any writing task with the resulting text a clear and neutral treatment of the issues, regardless of one's own particular personal opinions related to the task</u>. No one expects any less from you in any of your professional writing.

As mentioned elsewhere, neutrality is relevant not only for restraining an overly negative approach, but also for preventing an overzealous treatment of the issues. The writer should not stray far from the middle line of neutrality, so that the readers can see clearly for themselves that the issues were treated in a fair and balanced perspective, and that all possible aspects were given their due consideration. The readers should be allowed to determine for themselves what the best solution is; the facts should speak for themselves. Unfounded criticism has no place in the professional writer's text, since ultimately this is just another form of unsubstantiated opinion. Further, it is inappropriate to lead the reader to unwarranted conclusions, sometimes by trickery and deceit. If the arguments you support cannot stand on the facts that you have available, then it is likely that they are simply not worth supporting at all.

Finally, even if you do disagree, find faults, have substantiated criticism, and so forth, it is always best to take a positive constructive approach, suggesting where good things have been observed, and how to improve upon those areas that need work. Every negative can usually be said more constructively in a positive manner in a way that reinforces the good that has been done, and encourages, rather than discourages, the reader.

Examples.

Bad: Though the overall idea was fine, your details were awful, style irresponsible and conclusions totally groundless.
Good: **Your basic idea was fine, but we need to improve on the structure of your presentation.**

Bad: I can't believe that you really can even think such a thing, let alone state it openly on paper for everyone to read.
Good: **I do not agree with your conclusions. If you consider these issues....**

Bad: I have been forced to collect donations to pay for flowers for Mrs. Breer's husband, who has recently entered a narcotics dependence rehabilitative program. If you really support this, you can contact me.
Good: **I am collecting donations to pay for flowers for Mrs. Breer's husband, who has recently entered a narcotics dependence rehabilitative program. Please help in any way that you can.**

Bad: In the worse case of the ignorant writer, the use of the term "Chinese" for the language(s) spoken in Taiwan reinforces the mistaken belief that all Taiwanese speak the same language.
Good: **The use of the term "Chinese" for the language(s) spoken in Taiwan can reinforce the incorrect perception that all Taiwanese speak the same language.**

Bad: Anyone who believes that the solution proposed by Miller is the answer must be as crazy as Miller himself.
Good: **The solution Mr. Miller proposed is unworkable in its present form.**

PLAIN WRITTEN ENGLISH for Business and Technical Applications, Main Text

Author and Edited by: Dr. Peter M. Skaer, Babel University Professional School of Translation

Published by : Babel Press USA
                 Babel Corporation
                 Pacific Business News Bldg. #208,
                 1833 Kalakaua Avenue, Honolulu,
                 Hawaii 96815

Copyright © BABEL Corporation 2014

www.ingramcontent.com/pod-product-compliance
Lightning Source LLC
Chambersburg PA
CBHW070402240426
43661CB00056B/2506